The author of this text
is not a registered Freemason and
has no religious affiliation.
The author is an independent
researcher who continues his pursuit
of understanding the sciences of life.

This book is one man's attempt at putting the
puzzling pieces of this life together
and trying to make sense of the whole thing.

Pi &
The English Alphabet
Vol. 1

A B C D E F G H I J K L M
N O P Q R S T U V W X Y Z
1 2 3 4 5 6 7 6 5 4 3 2 1

by Marty Leeds

"*The Universe* is the *game of the self*, which plays hide and seek forever and ever."
~ Alan Watts

CONTENTS

"Thou hast the power of taking thought, of seeing it and grasping it in thy own *hands* and gazing face to face upon God's Image. But if what is within thee even is unmanifest to thee, how, then, shall He Himself who is within thy self be manifest for thee by means of outer eyes?"
~ Hermes Trismegistus
The Corpus Hermeticum

"One is filled with admiration...at seeing a doctrine so logical, so simple and so absolute. The necessary union of ideas and signs, the consecration of the most fundamental realities...a philosophy simple as the alphabet, profound and infinite as the Word; theorems more complete and luminous than those of the Pythagoreans; a theology summed up by counting on one's fingers."
~ Albert Pike, 33rd degree Feeemason
(Excerpt from *Morals and Dogmas* - speaking of the Kabbalah)

"The world is made of words and if you know the words the world is made of, you can make of it whatever you wish."
~ Terence McKenna

"When confronted with decimal places, the Great Triune Spirit will invariably *round up*."
~ Claudia Pavonis

"Death - I say? There is no death. Only a change of worlds."
~Chief Seattle

"Merrily, merrily, merrily merrily...*life is but a dream*."
~ "Row, Row, Row Your Boat," English Nursery Rythme

To be one ask "One."

INTRODUCTION

Gematria is the ancient art of assigning numbers to letters to reveal deeper meaning and significance to words. Gematria has been used for centuries, most notably by the Hebrews through the Kabbalah. Cryptograms and ciphers for languages have been used by the Greeks, Hindus, Egyptians, Freemasons and alchemsists for ages. Most of the religious texts that have been passed down to us utilized homonyms, symbols and ciphers in the language of the stories to wholly encompass, through the merging of mythology and history, the unifying principles that ruled the cosmos. Characters and events embodied ideas and concepts of divine import. Fundamental universal truths and principles became evident by understanding the language, symbols and mathematics encoded in these stories. Many view these texts and stories as either historical fact or pure fiction. Hardly ever are they understood for their true meaning.

Gematria is, essentially, a lost art. This esoteric discipline, when intuited and utilized, elucidated the most profound truths hiding within the lines of scripture. A true interpretation of books such as the Zohar and the Holy Bible could never be fully realized without understanding this ancient art. Those who studied the Kabbalah shared the idea that language was built upon the foundation of number and therefore, letters themselves should be represented by numbers. The word "Gematria" is derived from the Greek and Hebrew word "geometry", meaning "earth-measure." Gematria was the synthesis of number, geometry, symbol, sound, astrology and language. It was the "Wholly Science." The ancients made no divisions in their study of the natural world for all was one and one was all. Many consider sciences like astrology and gematria to be the result of superstitious, over-imaginative, archaic minds. Modern scientists tend to start their investigations with the enormous bias that the entire universe started with a massive explosion that has no real reason or inherent purpose for its existence. Is the picture they paint correct? So many cultures have shared in common the belief of a higher power or great spirit. No matter what language these cultures spoke (currently there are over 6,000 in use today), a vast majority of them had a term for divinity or god. Number is the one language that bridges all of these cultures and languages. Did our ancestors perchance understand that all languages, at their very essence, had an underlying structure, cipher or key that could unveil the power of the divine within our speech? Many of these ancient cultures saw god every which way they looked, in everything from the lights in the sky to the cold hard ground. They heard it in every word that was spoken.

1

THE WHOLLY RATIO OF PI

"If why is the question, Pi is the answer." - Claudia Pavonis

Pi has long been defined as the ratio of a circle's circumference to its diameter.

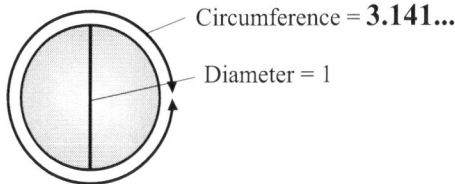

Circumference = **3.141...**

Diameter = 1

A mathematical constant represented by the Greek letters:

πΠ

Pi is an infinite, transcendental and "irrational" number. Its decimal places never end and never repeat. Pi is a constant that has consistently plagued mathematicians for years. Why is it that a simple circle should yield us this endless string of irrational digits?

For ages, mathematicians have tried to "crack Pi." Is there a pattern within this seemingly illogical set of numbers? If we could find such a pattern, what would it mean? Kurt Goedel, an Austrian-American logician, who was awarded the Einstein Genius Award for mathematics, wrote of a simple idea he called "The Incompleteness Theorem". The Incompleteness Theorem explained that a closed system can not define its own axioms. Or in other words, if we are trying to measure a circle, we would need to be inside another larger circle in order to do that measuring and therefore could never truly measure a "perfect" circle because *we can never truly measure anything outside ourselves*. Pi is considered a *transcendental* number. Transcendental means "to climb over or surmount". Much like our Universe, Pi seems to be infinite, transcendental and yet held together perfectly. But is it *irrational*?

Maybe there is absolutely nothing "irrational" at all about Pi, maybe we have just forgotten how to think *rationally* about the problem. Maybe instead of trying to "crack Pi", we instead should try to put it back together. Maybe we need to speak its language.

LANGUAGE

What is language and when did it originate? Many modern scientists see language as nothing more than small mouth noises made by evolved primates. Language is often considered an epi-phenomenon of consciousness that developed merely as an evolutionary advantage. Contemporary science believes language evolved between 50,000 and 150,000 years ago - a range so wide it becomes meaningless. Why have there been so many different languages throughout time? How did they develop independently? Why are so many root sounds shared by different cultures, on different continents during different epochs of time? Language is a part of everything we do. Communication, thought and dreams are all often linguistically driven.

"In the beginning was the word and the word was with god and the word was god." - John 1:1, The New Testament, King James Bible. And ultimately that word "became flesh." What is this *word* that Saint John the Divine speaks of? "Word" comes to us from the Greek term, "Logos", which is defined as the animating principle pervading the universe. Logos literally translates to "symbol and ratio". The logos was the ever-evolving force that lived within every living thing. In the Corpus Hermeticum, the revered ancient book of Egyptian wisdom written by Hermes Trismegistus, "logos" was analogous to "reason". The Greeks deemed this force a "word" or a "symbol" and hence believed that it somehow did its magic through sound. Cymatics is the modern science of using sound to create structure and form. At the right vibration, sound will naturally form complex, often symmetrical, geometric patterns. The "universe" literally means "One line of poetry", or better stated, a *unified word*. The Hindu's believe the universe started with the all encompassing vibration of AUM that was symbolized by a **3**, with a tail swirling out of its back, which is most assuredly a reference to the ratio of PI or **3.141**.

God *saying* "let there be light" is yet another reference to all of creation being manifested by a word, utterance or sound. If sound itself is not only a symbol but also a ratio, then maybe understanding sound and words are the keys to understanding the universe. Maybe we have to look no further than the very words we speak to understand who we are, where we are going and why we are here.

FREEMASONRY

Freemasonry is a fraternal organization that arose from obscure origins in the late 16th to early 17th century. Freemasonry now exists in various forms all over the world, with a membership estimated at around six million. Outsiders have leveled all sorts of accusations at Freemasons: they've been associated with the Knight's Templar, the Rosicrucians, the New World Order, the Illuminati, holders of the Holy Grail, blood line descendants from Jesus Christ and the builders of the great cathedrals of Europe. They have been deemed evil, conspiratorial, angelic and everything in between. Who are these people and what are they doing behind closed doors? Why do they use so many symbols and what do their symbols mean? What do they know and what are they not telling us? Why do they have so many secrets and why is their influence seen worldwide? Many, if not all of the "founding fathers" of the United States were Freemasons. George Washington, Benjamin Franklin and Thomas Jefferson were all members. To study the history of the United States without studying Freemasonry would be an enormous oversight. Many of our state buildings, temples and even the Constitution itself is littered with masonic ideas and symbolism. How has their influence been so profound and yet the majority of our history books completely ignore this organization? The Freemasonic Brotherhood, *at its core*, was an organization dedicated to introducing an Entered Apprentice to a world of higher truths. The Freemasonic credo of "Making good men better" says it best. But one does not have to join a lodge to pursue the fundamental truths laid forth by great thinkers like Plato, Pythagoras and Hermes, just as one does not need to seek an organized religion to have communion with god. A Freemason is *one who builds his own destiny*. He builds *(mason)* freely *(free)*. Freemasonry is most noted for the symbol seen below, a compass lain atop of a square with the letter "G" inscribed between. What does this symbol mean and why is it so prominently used?

The Freemasons did not hide their secrets. They put them in view for all to see. As it turns out, their main symbol was the key to unlocking the gematria of the English Alphabet.

THE KEY

KEY
3 5 2 = **10**

The **10**
fingers
of our
hands

The 26 letters
of our
Alphabet

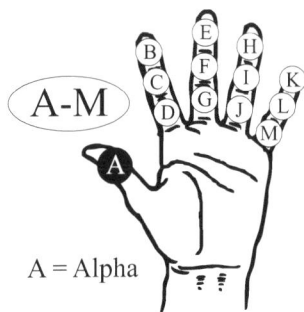

A-M

A = Alpha

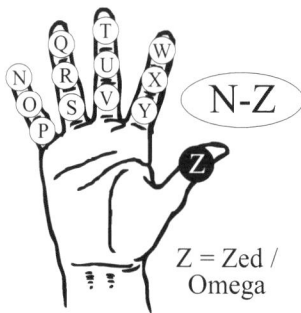

N-Z

Z = Zed /
Omega

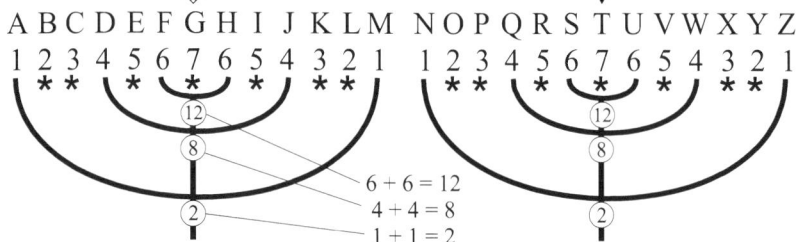

A B C D E F G H I J K L M   N O P Q R S T U V W X Y Z
1 2 3 4 5 6 7 6 5 4 3 2 1   1 2 3 4 5 6 7 6 5 4 3 2 1
* *   *   *   * *   * *   *   *   * *

(12)
(8)
(2)

6 + 6 = 12
4 + 4 = 8
1 + 1 = 2

(12)
(8)
(2)

$$2 + 8 + 12 = 22$$
$$22/7 = \pi \ (3.142...)$$

$$2 + 8 + 12 = 22$$
$$22/7 = \pi \ (3.142...)$$

---

* - Denotes Prime
Numbers
(Numbers divisible by 1
and themselves)

Prime numbers on left hand:
2 + 3 + 5 + 7 + 5 + 3 + 2 = 27

Prime numbers on right hand:
2 + 3 + 5 + 7 + 5 + 3 + 2 = 27

There are 27 bones in
the human hand

ה + ו + ה + י = (26)
He   Vov   He   Yod
5   6   5   10

THE TETRAGRAMMATON
The Holy Name of God in Hebrew
Translates to Jehovah
or YHWH

π 7 π 7

Pi begotten by 7 &
Pi begotten by 7

5

THE CIPHER

The numerical equivalents of the letters on the previous page can be easily abridged into the following cipher:

A B C D E F G H I J K L M
N O P Q R S T U V W X Y Z
1 2 3 4 5 6 7 6 5 4 3 2 1

We will be using this cipher throughout the text so taking the time to internalize this cryptogram is most advised.

There are 26 letters in the English Alphabet. The Tetragrammaton, known as Jehovah or YHWH, was a symbol used by the Kabbalahists, alchemists and Hermeticists and in the Hebrew gematria it added up to 26. (See "Helpful Resources" for the Hebrew alphabet and its numerical equivalents)

$$ה + ו + ה + י = 26$$

He   Vov   He   Yod
5   6   5   10

There is a direct correlation between the 26 letters of our alphabet and the Hebraic numerical equivalent of the Tetragrammaton. Tetra means "four" or the four characters making up the Holy Name of God and "gramma" means grammar. "Gamma" is a Greek term for light and one that is still in use today. *Gamma* is therefore light and *gramma* is sound and symbol and we will see the power of these two principles later in the text.

We see on the stained glass window shown below, from an Episcopal church in Iowa, built in 1868, the Tetragrammaton is slightly modified from the original Hebrew representation. Here the Tetragrammaton is symbolized as Pi 7 Pi 7.

The seventh letter of the English Alphabet is G. In the Freemason symbol we see that the G is encased by a compass and a square. The compass and square represent a common mystical mathematical problem celebrated throughout the ages known as "Squaring the Circle". We will revisit this concept in a bit, but in short, when one "squares the circle" of the Earth, one can find the radius of both the Moon and the Earth equaling **5,040** miles. Interestingly and absolutely not coincidental, if we multiply the numbers 1 through 7, we yield the number **5,040**. 1 x 2 x 3 x 4 x 5 x 6 x 7 = **5,040**. The G is of course the 7th letter of the alphabet and lo and behold, it is nestled between both a compass and a square.

The Freemasons accept all manner of faith into their organization but subscribe to the King James Holy Bible as their holy book. God was said to have created the universe in 6 days, resting on the 7th or the Sabbath. If we take this mythological motif and lay it upon the alphabet, we can assign numbers to the first 7 letters, A through G.

A B C D E F G H I J K L M
1 2 3 4 5 6 7

Resting on the seven, or the Sabbath, God's work was done and man's was about to begin. If we now fall back down the ladder of the alphabet, or from 7 back to 1, representing *the fall of mankind* from the Garden of Eden, we can assign numbers to half of the alphabet.

A B C D E F G H I J K L M
1 2 3 4 5 6 7 6 5 4 3 2 1

Falling back down to 1 in our alphabet has found us at the letter "M". M is the 13th letter of the alphabet which makes for a perfect division of the 26 letters of our entire alphabet. The next letter is of course "N" dividing our alphabet between M and N. The Alpha, represented by the "A" in our alphabet, was the first creation. If we insert the alpha into the natural division of our alphabet, we find the human race: **MAN**.

With the use of mirroring, or perfect symmetry, the numerical equivalents of the first half of our alphabet, A-M, can now be transferred to the second half of our alphabet, N-Z. This is best displayed on the human hands. The "A" or Alpha is one's left thumb and the "Z" or Zed, representing the end or Omega is one's right thumb with the 12 sections of one's four fingers, 24 total, representing the remaining 24 letters of our alphabet.

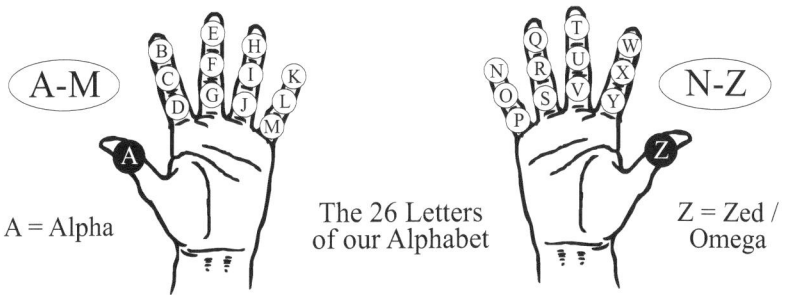

A-M

N-Z

A = Alpha

The 26 Letters
of our Alphabet

Z = Zed /
Omega

Now that we have the numbers for our alphabet we can pull out the prime numbers within our letters. Prime numbers are numbers that are divisible by only 1 and themselves. 2, 3, 5 and 7 are all prime numbers and are highlighted below.

A B C D E F G H I J K L M N O P Q R S T U V W X Y Z
1 2 3 4 5 6 7 6 5 4 3 2 1 1 2 3 4 5 6 7 6 5 4 3 2 1
  * *   *   *   *   * *   * *   *   *   *   * *

If we add up the prime numbers on each side of the alphabet they total **27**. 2+3+5+7+5+3+2 = **27**. This yields **27** for the left hand of our alphabet and **27** for the right hand. What is most interesting is that there are **27** bones that make up the human hand. Notice we have 7 prime numbers for each hand of our alphabet as well, with the central prime number, 7, paired with the letters G and T. "T", or the Tao Cross, is a symbol for man. It is a symbol that represents balance within the duality of the material word. The Freemasons used this cross often as seen in their amulets and rituals. We will explore this cross in depth in Volume 2 of this text.

We can now underline the non-prime numbers within our alphabet, 1, 4 and 6, and we can separate these numbers from the rest of our primes.

A B C D E F G H I J K L M   N O P Q R S T U V W X Y Z
1 2 3 4 5 6 7 6 5 4 3 2 1   1 2 3 4 5 6 7 6 5 4 3 2 1
– * * – * – * – * – * * –   – * * – * – * – * – * * –

By utilizing the ancient symbol of the Jewish Menorah on each half of our alphabet positioning the central 7s, G and T, as the pillars, we can derive the ratio of Pi. Notice below we connected the 1 and the 1, the 4 and the 4 and the 6 and 6 on each side of the alphabet with the branches of the menorah. 1+4+6+6+4+1 = 22. This 22 is connected by the central pillar of the menorah leading to the 7. A whole number approximation of Pi can be found by dividing 22 by 7 equaling 3.142. This yields us Pi begotten by 7 on the left hand of our alphabet and Pi begotten by 7 on the right hand of our alphabet. And this comes together to give you the Tetragrammaton, or the Holy Name of God.

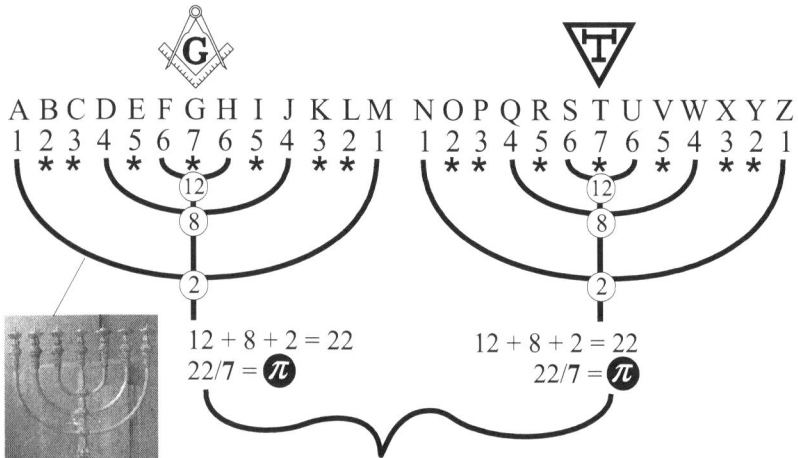

A B C D E F G H I J K L M   N O P Q R S T U V W X Y Z
1 2 3 4 5 6 7 6 5 4 3 2 1   1 2 3 4 5 6 7 6 5 4 3 2 1
  * *   *   *   *   * *   * *   *   *   *   * *
            12   12
             8   8
             2   2

$12 + 8 + 2 = 22$ $12 + 8 + 2 = 22$
$22/7 = \pi$ $22/7 = \pi$

π 7 π 7
Pi begotten by 7 &
Pi begotten by 7

TETRAGRAMMATON
The Holy Name of God
in Hebrew
Translates to Jehovah
or YHWH

9

FINDING AND REDEFINING GOD

How often is it that we hear people express their love and gratitude for God and yet how often do we hear people curse the very idea of this great being? For every devout follower there is another who laughs at the very idea. All sorts of communions and divisions are made on behalf of this "Great Spirit". The adherence to a particular faith and particular interpretation of the many holy books that are attached to this all powerful being has lead to wars and horrendous torturous acts as well as to revelations and renaissances. Many people, often reading from the same religious text will tell you that "God loves you" and that you should simultaneously "Fear God". How are we to come to any common ground with such varying degrees of interpretations and definitions? What is the impulse that drives mankind to believe in such a being? A vast majority of the cultures that have shared this Earth with us believed in a "great spirit" or "divine power". Did these cultures believe in God because they were primitive? Whatever their drive, adoration for this being has effected every moment of history.

How does one define this great spirit or great mystery? God has been given numerous names and yet been called "Unnameable". This mysterious being has been said to live in the heavens as well as in one's very own soul. In order to understand this great spirit, one must first understand the limitations of human thought. The comparative mythologist and author Joseph Campbell stated that "God is a metaphor for that which transcends all levels of intellectual thought. It's as simple as that." In the Egyptian lore, Isis, the mother goddess of all creation expressed that "No mortal man hath ever me unveiled.". If we cannot ever "unveil" this great being or spirit, how are we to know what he/she asks of us? How are we to know this being even exists? The great philosophers of the ages knew that man had limits to how far his thoughts could reach. Isis's veil, in one allegorical sense, was the curtain veiling God that no human eyes could bare to see. It was the wailing wall in one's own head that could not be surmounted. In the dark, cavernous abyss of mind is where the ultimate questions existed. Who are we? Why are we here? What is the meaning of life? Paradoxically though, it was exactly in this place that through meditation and contemplation the ultimate truths of existence could be grasped. In the dark and scary recesses of one's mind, the truth of God waits to be found.

Countless sermons, books, manuscripts, poems and stories have been written about God. Civilizations have built entire cities, stone circles, pyramids and earthen mounds based around their love for this great being. Books such as the Holy Bible, the Zohar, the Koran, the Mahabarata, the Upanishads and the Te Tao Ching have existed for centuries ruminating on the nature of being and the nature of the holiest of holies. God and his works have been etched onto pages century after century and thankfully these pages have lasted long enough for us to receive their enlightened words.

How can we come to know God? How can we find proof of this Great Spirit's existence? On a clear night, all one has to do is look up at the banner of stars above our heads to answer those questions. One has to look no further than down at one's own two hands to see the magical works of God.

The peoples of the past knew that in order to understand the glory of the universe, one first needed to understand one's self. The Delphic Oracle, the most important oracle in the Greek pantheon, says to "Know Thyself". How well do we truly know ourselves? How often is it that we stop and count the number of sections on our fingers? How often is it that we stop and examine the very words we speak? How often do we measure our own human bodies or ponder at how they are constructed? How often do we interpret our dreams? Maybe in order to understand the nature of God, maybe all we need to do is understand ourselves, the Earth we live on, the Sun above our heads, the measure of our bodies, the numbers we work with and the words we speak. And in doing this, perhaps we'll find God *within us.*

"If those who lead you say to you, 'See, the kingdom is in the sky, then the birds of the sky will precede you. If they say to you, 'It is in the sea,' then the fish will precede you. Rather, *the kingdom is inside of you*, and it is outside of you. When you come to know yourselves, then you will become known, and you will realize *that it is you who are the sons of the living father.*"
~ The Gospel of Thomas, verse 3

God is neither distant nor distinct from you."
~ Bhagavan Sri Sathya Sai Baba

ALCHEMY

The practice and study of alchemy has caught the eye of some of the most prominent and ingenious minds throughout history. Isaac Newton, the father of the modern scientific method, was himself a practicing alchemist. Alchemy's origins are unknown, but many believe its birthplace was in Egypt. The Arabic name for Egypt was Khemet, or the black land, and the magical arts practiced there came to be known as Al Khemet. Alchemy, simply put, is the study of the self. It is the willfull trans-substantiation of the human soul. It is melting and remelting, casting and recasting, forming and reforming the essence of the human soul until the elusive "philosopher's stone" is formed. This stone was said to be the seat of the soul and on the seat of the soul (known as the Merkabah in Jewish mysticism) sat you as a representation of the entire universe. Finding the philosopher's stone meant that you fully realized through trial and error, philosophy and psychology, science and reason, mysticism and mythology, mathematics and measure, that you, the alchemist were in fact, God himself. And this deep understanding of the nature of reality is how we ended up with phrases like "As above, so below", or "On Earth as it is in Heaven." This is not mystical nonsense, but a fundamental truth within cosmic law. The philosopher Alan Watts once said, "The further and further we look out with our telescopes and the further and further we look in with our microscopes, the larger and larger or smaller and smaller the universe has to become in order to escape the investigation because we are the universe looking at itself". The alchemists understood that there can be no division between you and the universal energy that manifests existence. We understand this today through the science of quantum physics and the "observer effect". The observer effect refers to the fact that the simple observation of a phenomenon will ultimately change the results of the phenomenon observed, or in other words, *all is connected*. This knowledge was the ancient secret of all ages. It is was what was taught in the mystery schools of Egypt and Greece. It is the message that is painted on cathedral walls, carved into temples, drawn as symbols, made into mythology and crafted into ritual. If one understood that he was in fact, a representation or an "undivided section" of the whole lot, one could design his life however he saw fit. This philosophy is analogous to the idea of a Freemason, or "One who builds his own destiny." Alchemy is, contrary to popular belief, a science. It is recognizing the divine within and without and understanding that divisions are illusory and the result of animal ignorance. Alchemy understood that the power of the world works in circles and therefore the whole cosmos and God was ultimately ONE and the circle was its symbol.

Black Elk, a Lakota elder reminded us that "The world works in circles and everything tries to be round". The circle is the most revered ancient symbol next to the cross. Used by pagans, druids, Norsemen, Christians, Hebrews, Islamists and native tribes and cultures throughout the world, the circle represented unity. A circle encapsulates the largest amount of space with the least amount of effort. The Greek Monad, which was the same symbol as the Egyptian sun glyph (seen below), is nothing more than a point placed in the center of a circle. The Greek Monad in their gematria added up to 361, or better stated, 360 degrees plus you in the center. One can easily see this symbol as representing nothing more than the point of a compass and the circle the compass creates when turned 360 degrees. This symbol meant wholeness and divinity. The stars above our sky and the Earth below our feet were one unified being. The Lakota natives had similar ideas and symbols as those of the Egyptians. Lakota philosophy states "That which is in the stars is also on Earth and that which is on the Earth is also in the stars." How is it that two cultures, separated by thousands of miles and an enormous ocean, came to similar conclusions? Notice the similarities between the man stretched over top of the scene in the Egyptian Stele (#666 from the Boulak Museum in Cairo, Egypt), the man stretched over the cross in the Lakota sand painting and the Milky Way as it stretches over our night sky. Through their symbols and philosophies, the Egyptians and Lakotas were passing down to us one of the most profound truths of the anicents: *Man is the cosmos.*

The Greek Monad and Egyptian Sun glyph.

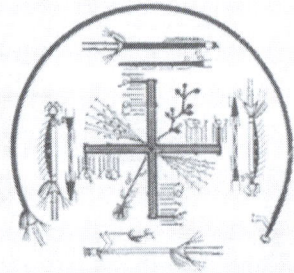

SQUARING THE CIRCLE

Squaring the Circle has long been revered as the ancient geometrical problem. The problem arose with the need to find the area of a circle. The solution was to find a formula or geometric construction that would enable someone to draw a square with an area that exactly corresponded to the area of a particular circle. The difficulty of this problem has been coined in the alchemical lore as "Squaring the Circle", a euphemism for something that was almost impossible and yet, mystical.

The ancient Egyptians identified certain pairs of whole numbers, 8 and 9 mainly, that came fairly close to squaring the circle. A circle with a diameter of **9** units almost corresponds in area to a square with sides of **8** units. The Great Pyramid of Giza's proportions fit within the squared circle below (the missing capstone would strike the heart of the moon, its base resting on the equator of the Earth). The Freemason symbol, as we have said, is an expression of this ancient idea. The compass represents Heaven pointing upwards and the square represents our Earth, pointing downward. These instruments symbolized the idea of "As above, so below.". In sacred geometry, Heaven was represented by a circle as the number 3 and Earth was represented by the number 4, as a square. The numerical equivalent of "Multiply" is 16275322. If you multiply these numbers together they equal **5,040**.

MULTIPLY
1 6275322   (1 x 6 x 2 x 7 x 5 x 3 x 2 x 2 = **5,040**).

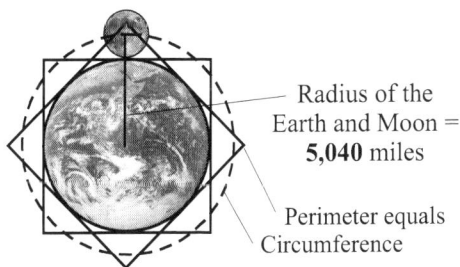

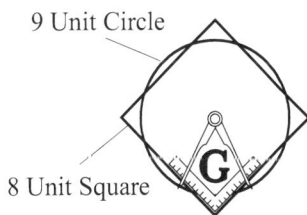

Radius of the Earth and Moon = **5,040** miles

Perimeter equals Circumference

9 Unit Circle

8 Unit Square

SQUARING THE CIRCLE

Area of a circle of 9 (4.5 Radius) Units : π x radius^2 = 63.64
Area of a square: 8 x 8 (or 8^2) = 64
1 x 2 x 3 x 4 x 5 x 6 x 7 = **5,040**
7 x 8 x 9 x 10 = **5,040**

$\cong$

14

THE GOLDEN PROPORTION

The Golden Proportion, also known as the Golden Mean or Golden Ratio, is a ratio that is present all throughout nature. The Greeks identified this ratio as the number 1.618. The total length "a + b" is to the length of the longer segment "a" as the length of "a" is to the length of the shorter segment "b".

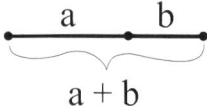

a + b is to a as a is to b   1 + .618 is to 1 as 1 is to .618

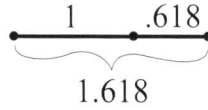

This proportion is expressed in the human body. From the bottom of your feet to your navel equals 1 and the navel to the top of your head equals .618, making you, the complete man, approximately 1.618. From your elbow to your wrist equals 1 and your wrist to the end of your middle finger equals .618, making your complete arm, roughly 1.618. This ratio was called "Phi" by the Greeks (with the lesser ratio being called "Phee") and was symbolized by the following characters:

$$\Phi\varphi$$

A five / Phive sided star or pentagram encodes this same ratio. The length of the longer segment of the star is 1 and the smaller segment .618. The pentagram is a widely used symbol in Christianity, Wiccan and pagan religions.

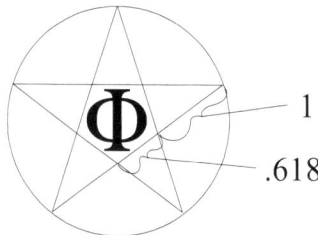

The Golden Proportion, or the number 1.618, can also be found hiding within the Fibonacci Sequence.

The Fibonacci Sequence is a sequence that was rediscovered in the 13th century by the French mathematician Leonardo of Pisa, also known as Leonardo Fibonacci. The sequence was originally formed to calculate how rabbits multiply when they mate. The series grows accruing terms that come from within itself, taking nothing from outside the sequence of growth. This pattern spirals as it grows to fruition. This spiral pattern is evident all throughout nature: tornadoes, sunflowers, ocean waves and pine cones all form from this fundamental sequence. From the first term, 0 the Fibonacci Sequence grows by simple addition as shown below.

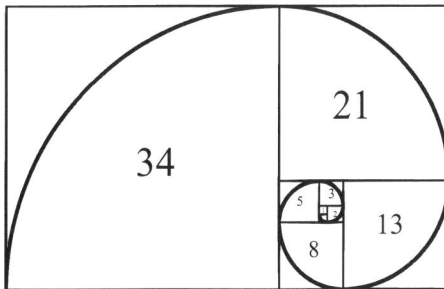

$$0 + 1 = 1$$
$$1 + 1 = 2$$
$$2 + 1 = 3$$
$$3 + 2 = 5$$
$$5 + 3 = 8$$

Decimal
Parity
Reduction

$$8 + 5 = 13$$
$$13 + 8 = 21 \quad (1+3) = 4$$
$$21 + 13 = 34 \quad (2+1) = 3$$
$$34 + 21 = 55 \quad (3+4) = 7$$
$$55 + 34 = 89 \quad (5+5) = 1$$
$$89 + 55 = 144 \quad (8+9) = 8$$
$$\quad (1+4+4) = 9$$

0, 1, 1, 2, 3, 5, 8, 13, 21, ,34, 55, 89, 144...
4   3   7   1   8   9

In order to find the Golden Ratio all one needs to do is take a number that occurs late in the Fibonacci Sequence and divide it by its predecessor (Example: 144 / 89 ≅ 1.618)

Decimal Parity, which is also known as Kabbalahistic reduction or Pythagorean addition, is the mathematical concept of adding numbers of the sum together to any make any number 1 - 9. Example: **42** would be $4 + 2 = $ **6**. Therefore **42** => **6**. Example: **29** would be $2 + 9 = 11$ and $1 + 1 = $ **2**. Therefore **29** => **2**. This idea is shunned by modern mathematicians but is an idea that was used by numerologists and astrologers of old. We can apply this concept to the Fibonacci Sequence and find a repeating sequence of numbers:

(0), 1, 1, 2, 3, 5, 8, 4, 3, 7, 1, 8, 9, 8, 8, 7, 6, 4, 1, 5, 6, 2, 8, 1

The first 24 numbers of the Fibonacci Sequence - before Decimal Parity reduction: 0, 1, 1, 2, 3, 5, 8, 13, 21, 34, 55, 89, 144, 233, 377, 610, 987, 1597, 2584, 4181, 6765, 10946, 17711, 28657

This cycle repeats itself ad infinitum with only one variation. The first 24 numbers, counting Zero as an arithmetical unit, sum to **108.** Every cycle beyond the first sums to **117**. The difference is caused by the first term in the sequence which is a zero in the first cycle but becomes a 9 every cycle thereafter. (0/9)

(0,) 1, 1, 2, 3, 5, 8, 4, 3, 7, 1, 8, 9, 8, 8, 7, 6, 4, 1, 5, 6, 2, 8, 1 = 108
(9,) 1, 1, 2, 3, 5, 8, 4, 3, 7, 1, 8, 9, 8, 8, 7, 6, 4, 1, 5, 6, 2, 8, 1 = 117

The Jewish Menorah can also be used to connect Zero and the numbers divisible by a Trinity (or 3, 6 and 9). The central pillar of the Menorah, in this exercise is 9, which is the Decimal Parity reduction of the number **144**. **144** *is the only square number in the Fibonacci sequence.* The Seven-branched Menorah and its central pillar of 144 are encoded within at least two verses of St. John's "Revelation": 1:12 - "And I turned to see the voice that spake with me. And being turned, I saw *seven golden candlesticks*." 7:4 - "And I heard the number of them which were sealed: *and there were* sealed a hundred *and* forty *and* four thousand of all the tribes of the children of Israel."

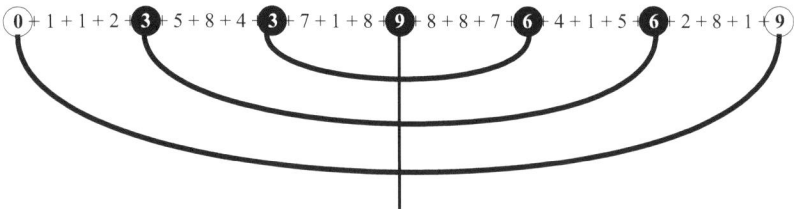

0 + 1 + 1 + 2 + **3** + 5 + 8 + 4 + **3** + 7 + 1 + 8 + **9** + 8 + 8 + 7 + **6** + 4 + 1 + 5 + **6** + 2 + 8 + 1 + **9**

When the first cycle of the Fibonacci Sequence, or our **Holy 108,** is placed around a circle it creates the most interesting diagram. We will see this again later in the text. Study of this symbol is highly suggested.

0 + 1 + 1 + 2 +
3 + 5 + 8 + 4 +
3 + 7 + 1 + 8 +
9 + 8 + 8 + 7 +
6 + 4 + 1 + 5 +
6 + 2 + 8 + 1 = **108**

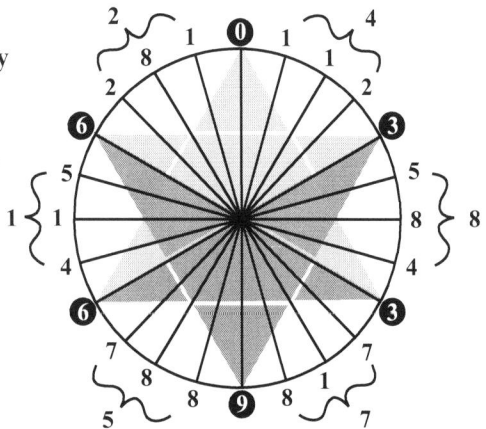

THE HOLY 108

There are 54 letters in the Sanskrit alphabet, and each has masculine and feminine (shiva and shakti) qualities.   54 times 2 is **108**.

The Indian Subcontinent rosary, or set of mantra counting, has **108** beads.

In the Krishna tradition, there were said to be **108** gopis of Krishna

The radius of the Moon is **1,08**0 miles.

The number **108** is used in Islam to refer to God.

The Chinese Buddhists and Taoists use a **108** bead mala, which is called su-chu, and has 3 dividing beads, so the mala is divided into three parts of 36 each.

The Sikh tradition has a mala of **108** knots tied in a string of wool, rather than beads.

There are 9 planets in the Solar System and 12 ages of the Zodiac.
9 x 12 = **108**.

Atman, the human soul or center, goes through **108** stages on the journey.

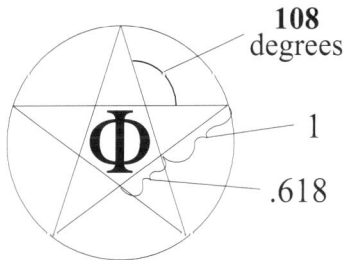

108
degrees

1

.618

Five - "Phive"

Using our cipher, the words "Add, subtract, multiply and divide" sum to **108**.

ADD SUBTRACT MULTIPLY AND DIVIDE
1 4 4   6 6 2 7 5 1 3 7   1   6 2 7 53 2 2 1   1 4   4 5 5 5 4 5 = **108**

Freemasonry has 33 degrees which are separated by 3 levels. Those levels are Entered Apprentice, Fellow Craftsman and Master Mason. See below how the numbers of the Golden Mean appear when we take the difference of the numerical equivalents of these three titles.

MASTER MASON
1 1 6 7 5 5   1 1 6 2 1 = 36
           The difference being **16**

FELLOW CRAFTSMAN
6 5 2 2 2 4   3 5 1 6 76 1 1 1 = 52

ENTERED APPRENTICE
5 1 7 5 5 5 4   1 3 3 5 5 1 7 5 3 5 = 70
           The difference being **18**

1.618
Phi Φ

The numbers 16 and 18 are interesting numbers in that, if one makes a 4 x 4 square equaling 16 and one makes a rectangle of 3 x 6 equaling 18, each one of these shapes will have a perimeter equal to its area. There are no other natural numbers with this property. The Platonists regarded this as a sign of their peculiar properties and Plutarch notes it when writing that the Pythagoreans considered 17 "utterly abominate" because it separated 16 and 18 and barred "them off from each other and disjoins them." The arab alchemist Jabir ibn Hayyan, known as Geber, in contrast to the Pythagoreans believed 17 to be the numerical basis of the physical world. We might be able to bridge this numerical conundrum using our cipher:

PEACE   MAGIC
3 5 1 3 5 = 17   1 1 7 5 3 = 17

...12 13 14 15 **16** ✗ **18** 19 20 21...

1.618
Phi Φ

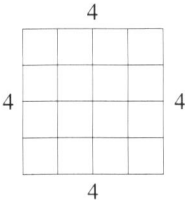

4 x 4 = 16 & 4 + 4 + 4 + 4 = 16
Area and Perimeter are equal

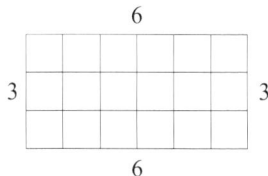

3 x 6 = 18 & 3 + 6 + 3 + 6 = 18
Area and Perimeter are equal

"Whoever cultivates the golden mean avoids both the poverty of a hovel and the envy of a palace."
~ Horace

HEAVEN & EARTH

Almost every culture around the world identified the stars above their heads as Heaven and the ground below their feet as Earth. History paints the story that a mere few hundred years ago, man believed the Earth was flat. We have all heard of Christopher Columbus fearing he would sail off the edge of the Earth on his voyage to the new world. Our are historical accounts accurate? It's hard to believe that people who navigated the oceans using the positions of the stars above as their guide did not understand the cyclical nature of the cosmos. After all, if we remove the "G" from GROUND we end up with ROUND. Why are the concepts of Heaven and Earth so universal? Many of our ancestors were avid sky watchers and understood intuitively the motions of the heavenly bodies. Many cultures relied on the stars and the position of the Sun and Moon in the sky to know when to migrate for the winter months, plant crops and even the best times to copulate. Knowing the cyclical motions of the Earth, Moon and sky above could literally be the difference between life and death.

Using our cipher the word "Heaven" equals **23** and "Earth" equals **24**. This puts the difference between Heaven and Earth to be 1. This 1 represents you. 23 is an important number because the numerical equivalents of "natural", "beauty", "temple", "lotus", "chosen", "eleven", "occult" and "circle" all equal 23. The Lakota natives called their Great Spirit or Great Mystery "Wakan Tanka" and it equals 23. "Rebis", a word that was used often by the alchemists, (draped across the chest of the androgynous alchemist seen below) also equals 23. Heaven plus Earth equals 47. The compass in the original Freemasonic symbol was opened to 47 degrees. Half of 47 is 23.5, which is the axial tilt of the Earth (shown below):

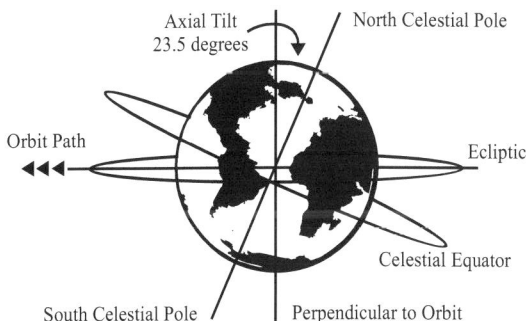

20

47 can be seen in the Tropic of Cancer and Capricorn. The Tropic of Cancer and the Tropic of Capricorn each lie at 23.5 degrees latitude. The Tropic of Cancer is located at 23.5° North of the equator and runs through Mexico, the Bahamas, Egypt, Saudi Arabia, India, and southern China. The Tropic of Capricorn lies at 23.5° South of the equator and runs through Australia, Chile, southern Brazil and northern South Africa. 23.5 + 23.5 equals 47.

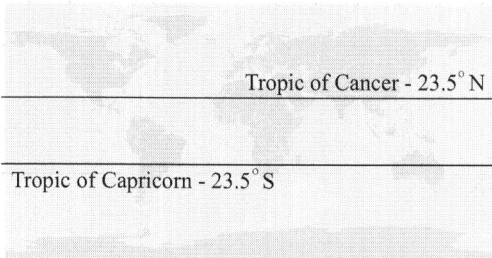

Tropic of Cancer - 23.5° N

Tropic of Capricorn - 23.5° S

Bohemian Grove, located in Northern California, is an exclusive gathering place for some of the world's most rich and powerful men. "Bohemian" equals **23** and "Grove" equals **24**, together summing to 47.

BOHEMIAN GROVE
2 2 6 5 1 5 1 1   7 5 2 5 5 = **47**

Adding the fist 6 digits of Pi together results in 23. 3+1+4+1+5+9 = **23**.

"Crack Pi" sums to **23** as well.   (3+5+1+3+3+3+5 = **23**)

23 also shows its face in the genetics of human beings. Human cells have 23 pairs of large linear nuclear chromosomes (22 pairs of autosomes and one pair of sex chromosomes), giving a total of 46 per cell.

The numerical equivalent of "The Holy Bible" equals 46.

THE HOLY BIBLE
7 6 5   6 2 24   2 52 2 5 = **46**

4 x 6 = 24. There are 24 hours in one Earth day. 4+6 = 10. Modern mathematics utilizes a base ten system. Mathematics is the one language that has permeated all cultures. Almost every tribe, religion, culture and civilization that we know of used a base ten system. Looking down at one's own hands will eradicate any doubts as to why they did.

Our cipher has "Earth" equaling 24. The Earth travels 24,000 miles in 24 hours. Could this be a coincidence? There are 24 major and minor keys in Western tonal music. Alchemy is the ancient process of turning lead into gold and there are 24 carats in 100% pure gold. We also saw that there were 24 numbers making up the Holy 108 in the Kabbalahistic reduction of the Fibonacci sequence. The radius of the Moon equals 1,080, or our Holy 108 x 10. If we multiply 1,080 by 24 we get the number 25,920, which is the length of time in years for the Precession of the Equinoxes (covered in depth further in this text). 1 through 4 multiplied equals 24 (1 x 2 x 3 x 4 = 24). There are 24 characters in the Greek alphabet. If we remove the A and Z in our alphabet, with A once again, representing the Alpha and the Z representing the Omega, or the end / zed, we're left with 24 letters.

There are 24 "eyes" in the sacred geometrical Flower of Life.

Words that equal 24: Heart, Egypt, Israel, Bishop, Sphinx, Pharaoh, Philos, Guru, Sacred, Flower, Savior, Passion.

Ra and Set, arch enemies in Egyptian mythology, add up to 24.
Ra being 6 and Set being 18 (6 + 18 = 24)

If we multiply "Heaven", or 6 x 5 x 1 x 5 x 5 x 1 and add that sum to the sum of the multiplication of "Earth", or 5 x 1 x 5 x 6 x 7, we get the number 1,800. (Heaven, 750 + Earth 1,050 = 1,800). An average adult heart pumps 1,800 gallons of blood in 24 hours. As it turns out, the merging of Heaven and Earth results in the pumping of your own heart.

THE COINCIDENTIA OPPOSITORUM

The Conicedentia Oppositorum, or Unity of Opposites, is a philosophical and scientific idea put forth by the famous Greek philosopher Heraclitus. Heraclitus understood that everything that existed in nature had an opposite. Man / Woman, Cold / Hot, Spirit / Matter, Wet / Dry, Good / Evil, etcetera. Most people recognize this philosophy from the popular Yin / Yang symbol.

There are essentially 3 dimensions of space, each with their opposites, Up / Down, Left / Right, Forward / Reverse. These 6 total dimensions of space, with *you, the observer*, being the axis or confluence of all these directions is mythologized in the 7 days of creation in Genesis. The word "Axis", viewed creatively, can be seen as "A", or the "Alpha", *meaning you*, and "six".

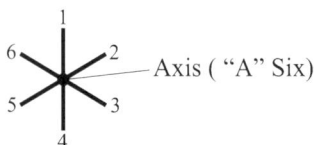

Axis ("A" Six)

God did all his mighty work in 6 days and then rested on the 7th day, or Sabbath. This is also one of the reasons that Sunday is considered a Holy Day, or a day of rest. The Sabbath is therefore nothing more than your point of view, or the seat upon which you view the world. And around this seat is a unity of opposites that spans 360 degrees.

Isaac Newton, the father of our modern sciences, noted that "For every action there is an equal and opposite reaction.", a direct reflection of Heraclitus' idea. Many modern scientists have enormous adulation for Newton because he solidified the scientific method, basing his discoveries and conclusions on reason, verifiability and repetition. What many do not know is that Isaac Newton spent much of his time deeply studying alchemy. Newton wrote volumes...handwritten page after handwritten page on the alchemical process. Alchemy is a science of the ages that our contemporary scientists see as the result of primitive, less-advanced minds. Newton gave us some of the finest scientific works of the last few hundred years. Through alchemy he helped us understand the duality of the natural world. Was Newton misguided, or *should we follow Newton's guidance?*

ALL DONE WITH MIRRORS

In Genesis, scripture says that God created the Heaven and the Earth, dividing the light from the darkness as well as creating day and night. This was done with a firmament that separated the waters from the waters. (Firmament means "sky" or "*vast dome*") If Heaven is the stars and space above our heads and the Earth the solid ground beneath our feet, why did the Bible choose to deem these things "waters"? In many cultures, Heaven was considered a reflection of Earth which in turn meant that Earth was indeed a reflection of Heaven. It is easy to see then why the Bible utilizes the term "waters." Anyone looking into water will see a reflection of themselves. One's right hand will become one's left hand. One's left eye becomes one's right.

At the Palace of Versailles in Paris, there is an infamous hall known as the "Great Hall of Mirrors". It is a highly decorated, fantastic piece of engineering and construction, all dedicated to the idea of reflection. Why did King Louie XIV go through all the trouble of making such a hall? Was it out of shear vanity or ego? Was King Louie merely obsessed with his outward appearance? Or did this great hall hold a much deeper symbolic significance? When someone goes to all the trouble of erecting a building of such complexity, we should realize that it is done with a very specific intention and is, without a doubt, richly imbued with meaning.

Everything in nature has mirror symmetry, or a reflection of itself within itself. One needs to look no further than the human body to see this phenomenon. Your feet, legs, arms, hands, breasts, ears and eyes are reflections of themselves. This is present in just about everything in the experiential world. This duality is how Mother Nature operates. It is her calling card. As we will see later in this text, the power of mirrors even works in the world of numbers. Numbers are not separate from nature and in fact are nature's language. Therefore, rationally, numbers themselves should be mirrored.

"The Holy Bible", as we have seen, sums to 46. With the application of mirroring 46 now becomes 64.

46 | 64

THE INFINITE NUMBER 64

The number 64 is a number that is seen all over the world. There are 64 hexagrams in the classic Chinese divinatory oracle of the I Ching, there are 64 squares on a chess board and there are 64 positions in the Kama Sutra. 64 is a number utilized in DNA, which is the chemical basis for all known living organisms. Without the self-replicating structure of the 64 codons in DNA, no life on this planet would exist. 64 is also seen in Marko Rodin's Vortex-Based Math (VBM), a mathematics that relies heavily on the Pythagorean addition. VBM creates an ever-looping, doubling and halving circuit that completes one doubling cycle in 6 moves, resolving at 64 (shown below). This doubling and halving, utilizing the number 64, was also used by the Egyptians in the Eye of Horus myth. In 3 and 4 dimensions, Marko's mathematics creates a torus; a shape that is seen in galaxies, hurricanes, typhoons and eddys in rivers. The Flower of Life, *the* ancient geometrical symbol, when shown in 3 dimensions, actually creates a torus as well by utilizing 64 spheres. The Flower of Life is seen all over the world, from Persia to China to India. 64 is nothing more than 8 squared (8x8). The character for 8 is the classic infinity symbol perched upright.

The symbol for 8 can also be viewed as a mobius strip, which is a single ring that is twisted making the outer section of the ring the inner section of the ring. In other words, it has one side and one edge.

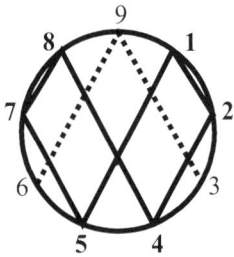

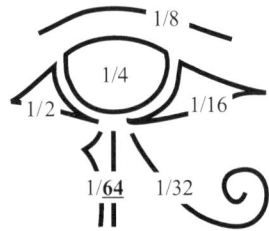

$$1$$
$$1 + 1 = 2$$
$$2 + 2 = 4$$
$$4 + 4 = 8$$
$$8 + 8 = 16 \ (1 + 6) = 7$$
$$16 + 16 = 32 \ (3 + 2) = 5$$
$$32 + 32 = 64 \ (6 + 4) = 1$$

Vortex-Based Math

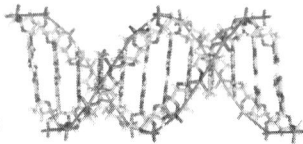

The Double-Helix structure of DNA

Eye of Horus

Mobius Strip

One of the most famous Alchemical illustrations, "Opus Medico Chymicum" created by the alchemist Johannes Daniel Mylius in 1618 (1.618!?), is shown below. The elements, symbols and ideas included in this masterwork are most profound. The numerical equivalent of "Opus Medico Chymicum" equals 64.

OPUS MEDICO CHYMICUM
2 3 6 6   1 5 4 5 3 2   3 6 2 1 5 3 6 1 = **64**

The four dimensions of geometry: point, line, plane and volume sum to **64** as well (18 + 13 + 12 + 21 = **64**).

POINT	LINE	PLANE	VOLUME
3 2 5 1 7 = **18**	2 5 1 5 = **13**	3 2 1 1 5 = **12**	5 2 2 6 1 5 = **21**

The 64th verse of the I Ching is one of the most recognizable verses and is indeed one of the most profound.

A tree as wide as a man's embrace grew from a tiny seed.
A tower nine stories high rose from a small heap of earth.
A journey of a thousand miles began with a single step.

THE PHILOSOPHER'S STONE

The philosopher's stone is the most elusive object in alchemical lore. The alchemist's task was to take a base metal, usually lead, and somehow transmute it into pure gold. This allegorical transmutation resulted in the forming of the philosopher's stone. What was this "object" that the alchemists venerated? The allegory of a chemical experiment was supposedly used as a means to ward off any impure seekers by veiling the true meaning of alchemy in something that might attract those who wished only for material wealth. The gold was the treasure of knowledge. This *treasure* was understood to be locked inside the *chest* of the spiritual man, who had a "heart of gold". The alchemist's temple is his own mind and body, the Holy Grail his own hands. This "stone of plenty" is the hardened realization that man is a divine being, crafted by a "great spirit" with a most sacred purpose. The alchemist is he or she who digs deep within the depths of him or herself, having the conviction and *faith* that the pursuit will ultimately bring them to the shores of a higher truth. This process takes the ignorant man or the animal-self and crafts him into a wise, loving and spiritual being.

The alchemical work, deemed the "Great Work" or "Magnum Opus" is the labor of the lord, the righteous path of the warrior and the hero's journey. It is analogous to the Bodhi path of the Buddhists, "The Way" of the Taoists and the search for enlightenment undertaken by every mystic and magi throughout the ages. It is the "one and only true way" that paradoxically has many paths. "The Way" to this knowledge is to travel through the heart and soul of oneself, through the milky waters of the galaxy of mind, to find one's higher purpose. It is journeying in to the depths of the self by journeying out to the stars, only to come to the realization that they are one and the same. The philosopher's stone was also sometimes known as the elixir of life. It was the substance of immortality. The "fountain of youth" sought after by so many seekers is most likely a mythological comparison to this alchemical substance. However this "object" or "substance" was ultimately symbolized, it was nonetheless powerful, divine and the key to the gates of one's personal heaven. There is little doubt that the work one had to undergo to receive this stone was done through number and symbol. The famous alchemist Michael Maier states in his work, *Atalanta Fugiens,* "Make of a man and woman a circle; then a quadrangle; out of the this a triangle; make again a circle, and you will have the Stone of the Wise. Thus is made the stone, which thou canst not discover, unless you, through diligence, learn to understand this geometrical teaching."

The metaphor of turning lead into gold was used deliberately for it has symbolic, psychological and numerical meanings. If understood, it could point one to the very essence of the fundamental truths of existence. Why was the process focused on lead and gold? Gold is a substance adored by many civilizations. Until very recently, America founded its entire monetary system on the "Gold Standard." Gold, with its shiny qualities and yellowish color, signifies the light of the sun that lies at the center of all things. The casing stones of the Great Pyramid of Giza were made of pure gold and it was said that at its pinnacle, the Great Pyramid could be seen shining across the landscape for miles. Its light represented the way of enlightenment or rebirth to one's higher, illumined self, a process that all humans must undergo to return to the glory of the kingdom of Heaven. Heaven, as we know, was symbolized by a circle and the number 3 by the sacred geometers of the ages. Pi is approximated with the number **3**.141 and is the ratio of a circle's circumference to its diameter. This "irrational" mathematical constant is, as we will see, the focal point encoded in many religious and mythological ideas. Alchemy is no different as we can see in the process of turning lead into gold.

LEAD   GOLD
2 5 1 4 = **12**   7 2 2 4 = **15**

The sum of "lead" equals 12 and the sum of "gold" equals 15. That puts two numbers between the two, **13** and **14**. With a little imagination, *the alchemist's finest tool*, we can mirror those numbers and get two numbers, 31 and 41. Combining these numbers and separating the Holy Trinity, or the heavenly number **3** with the decimal place, we yield that magical number of Pi, **3**.141.

The Holy Trinity is known in Hinduism as Shiva, Brahman and Vishnu, and well known by the Father, the Son and the Holy Spirit in Christianity. Even the title of the "Holy Bible" incorporates the all- encompassing number **3**. Bi, meaning two, and "El", meaning God, represent the Father and Son and the third part of the Trinity, being the "Holy" of the Holy Spirit. Holy is most definitely a homonym, for nothing is more transcendental and *WHOLLY*, than the ratio of Pi.

$$\pi\Pi$$

28

ADAM & EVE / ISIS & OSIRIS

When one understands that the myths that have been passed down to us are not intended to be taken as literal historical fact, the beauty of these stories unfold right before one's eyes. Many cultures have stories that have similar elements. One of those motifs is the idea of a man and woman being at the helm or forefront of all creation. The two most notable couples are the Egyptian Isis and Osiris and the biblical Adam and Eve.

The Isis and Osiris myth generally goes like this: Set, the arch rival of Osiris, cast Osiris into the Nile River in a sarcophagus only to later find him and cut him into 14 sections. Isis, Osiris' counterpart, went to retrieve the missing pieces but only recovered 13 out of the 14. The missing piece was said to have been eaten by a fish in the Nile River. Isis then fashioned a phallus out of gold to help resurrect Osiris, who was reborn and became lord of the afterlife. There are many elements encoded in this story such as the ideas of alchemical gold and spiritual rebirth, as well as the idea of the human body being measured by 14 sections of Phi and Phee (covered later in this text) to name but a few, but the one idea we will focus on here is the one that encodes Pi. Just like the lead into gold of alchemy, we are given the numbers 13 and 14 and just like we did before, all we need to do is mirror those numbers and once again place our decimal place after that mighty Trinity, and low and behold, we find Pi. **3.141**.

In the biblical myth, Adam and Eve were together in the Garden of Eden. They were equals and with the good lord until one day, a serpent came along and tempted them to eat from the Tree of the Knowledge of Good and Evil. God instructed them that if they did, they would surely die, but the temptation of "sin" was much too great. They took a bite from the apple and were cast out. Let's look at the numerical equivalents of these two mythological characters.

<table>
<tr><td>ADAM</td><td>EVE</td></tr>
<tr><td>1 4 1 1 = 7</td><td>5 5 5 = 15</td></tr>
</table>

Adam sums to 7 and Eve sums to 15. Adam and Eve combined therefore would equal **22**. There are 4 letters in Adam and 3 in Eve which make a total of **7** letters. 22/7 = 3.142, a close approximation of Pi using whole numbers. It would seem that no matter the creation myth, both man, woman and Pi are a central focus.

PRECESSION OF THE EQUINOXES

The Precession of the Equinoxes is a phenomenon known, mapped and revered by many ancient cultures throughout time. Precession is the slow continual drift of the stars against the backdrop of our night sky. The Egyptians, Sumerians, Mayans, and Hindus all recorded this movement and encoded it their temples and mythologies. The constellations of our night sky move in a retrograde motion 1 degree every 72 years. Since there are 360 degrees in a circle, the entire cycle should therefore take approximately 25,920 years to complete one rotation (72 years x 360 degrees = 25,920). This great span of time was known as the "Great Year" or "Platonic Year" by the Greeks and was divided into segments: the Gold, Silver, Bronze and Iron ages. Why was this large cycle so important to our ancestors? Since it takes 72 years, or basically a lifetime, for the stars to move a barely noticeable 1 degree, why would anyone go through the trouble of mapping this immense time span?

Precession was mapped because it was a cosmic clock. It was a macrocosm of the microcosm of our solar year here on Earth. It allowed the ancients to understand when great changes would occur on Earth, just as the Sun moving across our sky delineated Winter, Spring, Summer and Autumn. It was the grand clock of the entire universe. And since man is an "undivided section" of the universe, understanding these heavenly motions was quintessential to understanding mankind. They knew, as we often say, that "The Kingdom of Heaven resides in you." Therefore, knowing what time it was in heaven was of grand importance.

Below are several different ways we can segment this great cycle. Currently, we use a Zodiac of 12 "houses" or "ages" of 2,160 years for an age. Not coincidentally, the number 2,160 is also the diameter of the Moon in miles.

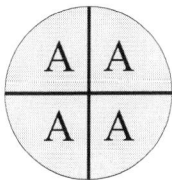

4 ages of
6,480 Yrs.

8 ages of
3.240 Yrs.

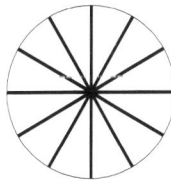

12 ages of
2,160 Yrs.

16 ages of
1,620 Yrs.

The twelve houses, ages or constellations of the Zodiac are shown below. Precession traces out an imaginary circle in the heavens every 25,920 years by the path of the North Celestial Pole. We will delve deeper into this phenomenon later in the text.

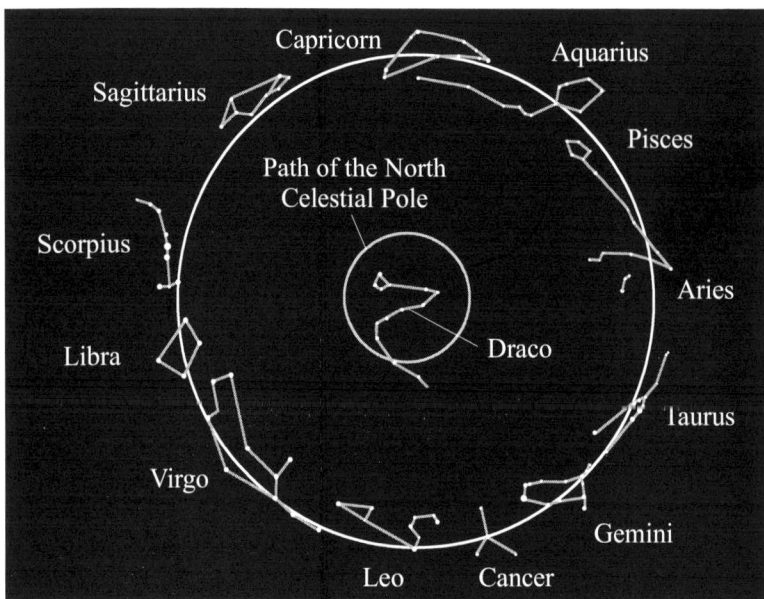

The word "time" itself encodes the 72 year shift of the one degree of the Precession of the Equinoxes. The numerical equivalent of "time" adds up to 18.

TIME
7 5 1 5 = 18

There are 4 letters in "time" equaling 18. 18 x 4 = **72**. The mirror of "time" is "emit".

| TIME | EMIT |

The definition of emit is "to give off light or heat" or "to give utterance or voice to". Therefore, the act of coursing through time in this human body is to give off light and give voice to the world. The function of time itself is to give rise to the magical show of sound and light that has woven us into existence.

THE 72 NAMES OF GOD

According to the Zohar, a holy book celebrated by followers of the Kaballah, there are 72 great names of God. There were said to have been 72 languages spoken at the Tower of Babylon. There were 72 disciples of Confucius. There were 72 conventional scholars who translated the Septuagint (a translation of the Hebrew Bible). 72 has made its way into the stories of so many cultures throughout the ages. As we have just learned, in the Precession of the Equinoxes, the stars move 1 degree every 72 years. This is undoubtedly why this number shows its face time and time again. One could keep track of the entire cyclic movement of the heavens by basically understanding this one number.

The alchemists who achieved the "Great Work" and received the infamous philosopher's stone were rewarded with the most profound realization: that man himself was divine, that all of the cosmos was constructed for him, before his own eyes and that all of the heavens above were but a mere reflection of the inner cosmos existing within the temple of man. Concepts such as this seem absolutely ridiculous to the minds of those who are intoxicated by physical existence and locked into a material view of our heavenly home. But no thought is more outrageous or absurd than the idea of this existence being the result of sheer accident. There is no thought more outlandish than believing that the perfected balance of this universe resulted from an unintelligent source. We came from stardust and possess higher consciousness and therefore, by proxy, stardust itself must be inherently intelligent and *conscious*. Is mankind simply adrift in a largely meaningless empty void? To this idea, the alchemist would laugh. The zen master would scoff.

If we add up the four ages of the Greek Platonic year, or Gold, Silver, Bronze and Iron, we get the number **72**.

GOLD   SILVER   BRONZE IRON
7 2 2 4   6 5 2 5 5 5   2 5 2 1 1 5 5 5 2 1 = **72**

If we add up the numerical equivalent of "Philosopher's Stone" we get **72** as well.

PHILOSOPHER'S STONE
3 6 5 2 2 6 2 3 6 5 5 6 6 7 2 1 5 = **72**

The Philosopher's Stone is indeed the concretized realization that man himself is the entire universe. Man is in fact, God, looking at himself.

THE ALL SEEING "I" OF GOD

Many know the "The All-Seeing Eye of God" (also known as "The Eye of Providence") from the back of a United States one dollar bill, which has an eye centered on a capstone that hovers above a pyramid (consisting of 72 stones with a 47 degree angle). This image is a powerful one. What does it mean? Does it symbolize an evil, vengeful God in the sky watching our every move? Does it represent the government's yearning to intrude into our life as an Orwellian "Big Brother"? This symbol is used consistently by the alchemists and Freemasons and has striking similarities to that of the Egyptian Eye of Horus.

| The Reverse of
The One Dollar Bill | The Eye of
Providence | The Eye of
Horus |

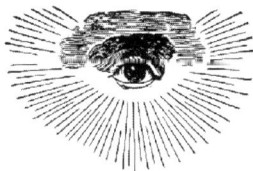

It takes but little effort of the imagination to understand the homonym used in this symbol. Phonetically, "Eye" and "I" are identical.

It is well known that cryptograms, ciphers and homonyms were used to represent multiple meanings encoded in the allegories of our mythologies. The devout spiritual seeker knew that the stories presented in all of our holy books, though they may have had some historical truths, were not intended to be taken literally. The story of a deluge, woven into the mythology of the Holy Bible, was undoubtedly an historical event - noted by thousands of flood myths told worldwide - but was not written down as to be the actual historical account of the events. This enormous oversight has deprived many religious followers from the splendid truths within these stories. These stories, when understood geometrically, numerically, philosophically and symbolically had the most profound meanings that could capture the heart of the most ardent disbeliever. By peeling away the layers of these stories, the symbolism, philosophy and magic within could *convert* even the most hard-lined skeptic. The All-Seeing Eye of God is a symbol that has many layers to its meaning but the one we will be concerned with is the one that concerns you the most.

The letter "I" in our cipher has the numerical equivalent of 5. Human beings are best represented by the number 5. There are 5 extensions of the body from the torso and humans have 5 senses; seeing, hearing, tasting, touching and smelling. There are traditionally 5 vowels in the English Alphabet (A, E, I, O, and U). The human body is constructed using the Golden Ratio of Phi, or "Phive", a ratio embedded in the geometry of the 5-pointed star or pentagram, as we have seen earlier. The symbol for Phi is an "I" that divides a circle.

$$\Phi$$

The circle of the "Eye" and the line of the "I" are references to the male and female. The circle is obviously feminine, symbolic of the womb or vagina and the line is symbolic of the phallus. These two symbols, combined in the symbol of Phi, represent the intersection of opposites in the world, necessary for the continuation of almost all species. Sexual union can be symbolized simply by a single line entering a circle.

The "eye" in The Eye of Providence also references the consciousness in man that allows him to have perspective and say "I". The eyes you use to view this page and the "I" of one's consciousness are universal. The "Eye" and "I" speaks of the universal mind that is inherent in all things from the inanimate to the animate. The next time you gaze at a rose or sunflower in your garden, notice that the head of that flower is circular and is looking directly at you while you look at it. It drinks up the morning dew, catches the sun's rays and reaches full bloom so you can appreciate it and it can appreciate you. You and the flower are the eyes of god looking at each other. The next time you walk by a tree in the park take notice of one of the knots in its trunk. This circular crack in its bark is not only reflective of the galactic bulge of our galaxy (the black hole located in the center of our galaxy being yet another eye) but also the "eye" it uses to see the world in which it branches out. How often have you looked into your own reflection with admiration? All things in nature have "eyes" as well as "Is". Everything is reflecting on everything else. And we have the ability, through language and symbol to understand the profundity of this universal event.

The All-Seeing Eye of God has its most profound meaning when one realizes that this symbol is not symbolizing some angry, judgmental god in the clouds, but instead the god who is holding this very book.

COMING UP "ONE" SHORT

In the classic study of gematria, most systems allowed for a difference of one. The Greeks for instance, when adding together the numerical equivalent of Monad, or 361, taught that the extra "one" was of no detriment and certainly not reason enough to recalculate one's math, even though a full circle is of course 360 degrees. This was not done because our ancestors were sloppy at math. Quite the contrary. This difference of "one" had a much more mystical meaning. Many mythologies and concepts utilized this missing or extra "one" for a very specific purpose. This "one" was intended to signify the person who was undergoing the symbolic, mathematical and geometrical understanding of the specific myth or concept. For instance, in the Egyptian lore, Horus, or "whole one" was fractured and the pieces of his eye were scattered across the sands of Egypt. When Thoth, patron of the arts and sciences, (and where we get the word "thought") went to retrieve the pieces of Ra, or Horus, he came up one short, making 63/64. In another Egyptian myth, Osiris, one of the most important deities in the Egyptian pantheon, was cut into 14 sections. When his counterpart, Isis, went to retrieve these pieces, she only found 13 pieces, coming up one piece short. In sacred geometry, as we have stated earlier, Heaven was known as a 3 as a circle, and Earth was known as a 4 as a square, with the difference being "one". In our cipher, "Heaven" equals 23 and "Earth" equals 24, with the difference being, once again, "one".

Our ancient ancestors, the master alchemists, the Egyptians, the Freemasons and the sacred geometers of the ages realized that one can not separate himself from the entire mystery of being because ultimately, he is the central focus of the entire mystery. They understood that the human being was made in the image of god, being intrinsically connected to the source of all things. We came from the first thing and we are the last thing the universe decided to do. Through billions of years of evolution, through the creation out of the chaos of the prima materia, man was crafted by the work of this "supreme being". The only way to make sense of the whole lot was to put oneself front and center to the mystery. One could not dismiss the observer observing the great mystery. The master craftsman of myths and lore utilized this idea in their mathematics because it was a necessary tool to aid man in understanding his place in the cosmos. It was done to elucidate the most fundamental truth of existence; that man's place is smack dab in the center of it all.

You are in fact, the missing or extra "one".

35

The sketch below is of the infamous archaeological, calendrical and ritualistic site of Stonehenge. These massive stones and their surrounding holes form an astrological calendar, mapping the cycles of the stars and heavenly spheres above. Yet Stonehenge has another purpose. Notice the "broken" or U-shaped set of stones in the center of the Sarsen Circle. These stones represent the "cracked egg", or the scission of our primordial egg, the egg that once encased all the potential of our manifested, experiential reality (An idea we will cover later in this text). When the initiate enters the stone circle and kneels at the "Altar stone", most likely a ritual would be performed to "alter" the state of the initiate, guiding him or her on the path to enlightenment. On the opposite side of the Sarsen Circle, a base-line can be drawn between the station stones on his or her left and right. Due North is roughly **138.5** degrees from this base-line. The degree of Philotaxis, the leaf arrangement around a plant, determined by the ratio of Phi, is **137.5** degrees. This is a difference of **1** degree. This degree represents the initiate's - and your - little slice of Heaven.

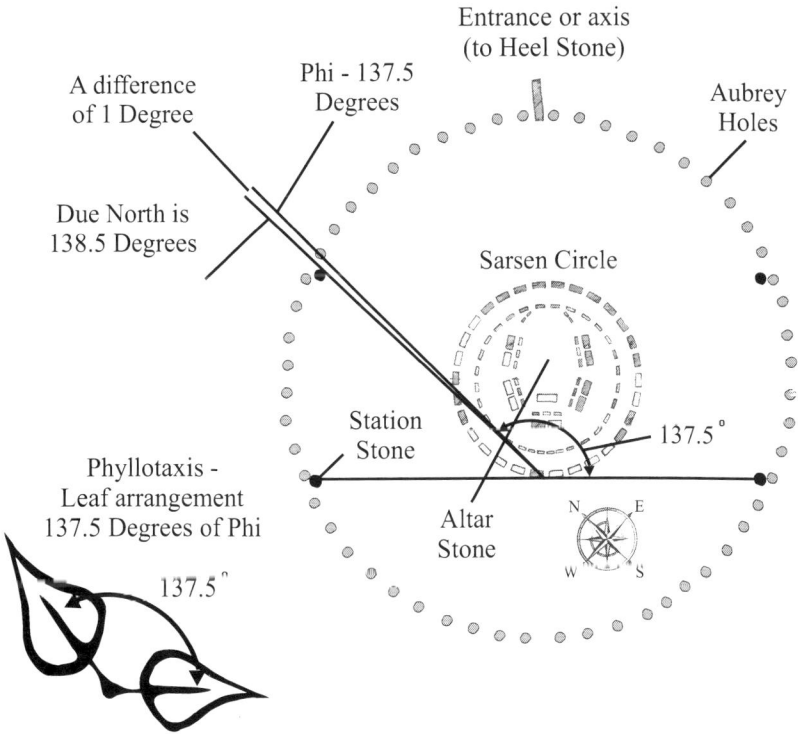

Entrance or axis
(to Heel Stone)

A difference
of 1 Degree

Phi - 137.5
Degrees

Aubrey
Holes

Due North is
138.5 Degrees

Sarsen Circle

137.5°

Station
Stone

Phyllotaxis -
Leaf arrangement
137.5 Degrees of Phi

Altar
Stone

N
E
W
S

137.5°

32 & 33 DEGREES

Freemasonry is based on a hierarchal system, structured in progressive degrees which the initiate or Freemason may ascend. Through hard work, study and *phi*lanthropy, the Freemason may slowly climb the ladder of illumination. Few ever reach the highest honor, or 33rd degree, and those who do seem to stake their place in history. Many of the political leaders of the world, including several United States Presidents, have climbed the ranks and achieved this most esteemed honor. An "Entered Apprentice" can reach the 32nd degree on his own accord but he must be "anointed" the 33rd degree by the Freemasonic "Supreme Council". Jesus Christ, formally Jesus of Nazareth, was said to have lived 33 years after performing 33 miracles. "Christ" literally means "The anointed one" and was a title given to Jesus after he had achieved illumination or enlightenment. Jesus had recognized that he was the "Son of God" or, better stated, he recognized the divinity that lay within him and therefore had himself reached this 33rd degree, mythologized by his age at death and the number of miracles he performed.

Jesus Christ was the "Son of God" and his life is the central focus of the New Testament. The Sun is located in the center of our Solar System and is the heavenly body around which all the planets revolve. Without the light or illumination of the sun, no life could exist. Jesus recognizing the light that existed within himself was the grandest of metaphors; it was intended to represent that all of creation revolved around the character and deeds of mankind. Jesus' life symbolized mankind's place as the pinnacle and center of all creation. Jesus' life was an example, like many of the other spiritually developed magis of the past, that one could identify with in order to find and understand the divinity within oneself.

Isaac Newton was the first person to elaborate the quantitative temperature scale with the invention of the thermometer. Newton defined the degrees from zero to 32 being the range at which water is frozen and the 33rd degree the temperature at which water unfreezes. Newton, as we have discussed, was an alchemist and the degrees between melting and freezing being 32 and 33 were certainly not chosen arbitrarily. 33 was a number revered by the Christians, Hermeticists and alchemists alike. It was a number that encoded and symbolized the divine fire that lay dormant within every individual.

The number 33 has a factorization of 3 and 11. This factorization represents the ratio of the Earth to the Moon with the Moon being 3 and the Earth being 11.

The Sun's core rotates once every 33 Earth days and the revolution of the surface of the Sun on itself occurs every 28 Earth days. The sun's core and its surface represent two different aspects of the same heavenly body. 28 plus 33 equals 61. The numerical equivalent of "The Holy Spirit" equals 61 as well.

THE HOLY SPIRIT
7 6 5 6 2 2 2 6 3 5 5 5 7 = **61**

The first 13 digits of Pi, when added together, sum to 61.

$$3 + 1 + 4 + 1 + 5 + 9 + 2 + 6 + 5 + 3 + 5 + 8 + 9 = \mathbf{61}$$

The numbers 28 and 33 represent two different aspects of the Sun. The political system of the United States is represented by two main political bodies, the Democrats and the Republicans. Democrat sums to 28 and Republican sums to 33. As it turns out, numerically, these two parties are, in all actuality, symbolizing one concept.

The Egyptian Hermes, who was often identified with Thoth, has a numerical equivalent of 28, representing the surface of the Sun. There has been much speculation by Egyptologists as to whether Hermes was the same figure or god as Thoth. The answer to this conundrum can be found in number. Both Thoth and Hermes add up to 28. 28 represents not only the surface of the sun but also (as we will see with the pillars of Jachin and Boaz) the number of days in a 13 month calendar. The character of Hermes was a man who married the opposites within himself (and where the terms "*hermetically sealed*" and "*hermit*" come from). The marriage of these opposites can be understood through the act of prayer. When one joins one's hands together, this symbolic act reflects the marrying of polar opposites, the opposites of course being one's left hand and one's right. There are 14 sections of one's 5 fingers, making the total number of sections for both hands 28. Therefore, the act of prayer is intended to connect oneself with the dualistic aspects that lay within the soul of oneself and is not an act meant to send one's thoughts out to an external God that exists in some distance place, far away from oneself.

Many important words and titles add up to the numbers 32 and 33.

Words that add up to 32:
Present, English, Lucifer, Freemason, Trinity, Axis Mundi,
King Solomon, Christ, Holy Grail, Gematria, Religion

Words that add up to 33:
Sirius, Orpheus, Preacher, Leviathan, Virtue, Triangle, History,
Knowledge, Common Sense

One of the most interesting words that sums to 33 is "clockwise".
Astrology is an ancient art practiced by many cultures of the past and one
that has been lost today. Many believe that astrology is merely an inter-
pretative practice assembled by primitive minds in order to give meaning
to one's existence. The movements of the planets and their positions
somehow affecting things here on Earth is widely considered ridiculous
by contemporary scientists. The peoples of the past shared the same
experience we share today. We are all born into the riddle of this existence
and straight answers seem hard to come by. We are all plagued with that
abyssal, eternal question, "Why"? The megalithic builders of the past,
those who constructed the Great Pyramids, Stonehenge and the cathedrals
of Europe were deeply in tune with their environment and understood much
more than we often give them credit for. Many of these ancient structures
focused on the cycles of the heavens above our heads. Stonehenge is in fact
a calendar written in stone. Time is the movement of all phenomenon. It is
the cathedral in which the drama of life is played out. Birth and death, decay
and growth all dance upon the stage of the great cycles of time. The
Kybalion, a classic book on Hermetic philosophy, states that, "Nothing rests;
everything moves; everything vibrates." Trying to keep stable in an ever-
moving world means that one must constantly go with the flow. The ever-
flowing way of the Taosist's "Tao" is the exact same concept. The mystics
of the past deeply understood that the movements of the heavens were anything but "random". Aligning oneself to these movements helped one understand the perfected, cyclical will of god.

Being "*clockwise*" is nothing more than having knowledge of time
itself. Wisdom and therefore gnosis seem to be linked directly with knowledge of the heavenly movements and the cycles of time.

JACHIN & BOAZ

Freemasonry celebrates the pillars of Jachin and Boaz as seen in many of their illustrations. These are the supposed pillars that stood on the porch of Solomon's Temple, the first Temple in Jerusalem. These pillars are often depicted with the Sun on one and a Moon on the other. Just like all the elements in Freemasonry and alchemy, these pillars represent many things; the gateway to a higher spiritual self and the entrance to the high wisdom of the ages as well as the cosmic duality or unity of opposites. What is most interesting about these pillars though, is that they point to a calendar used by many ancient cultures, cleverly encoded in many different ways.

JACHIN   BOAZ

4 1 3 6 5 1   2 2 1 1

The numerical equivalents of Jachin and Boaz add up to 26 - or the sum seen in the Hebraic Tetragrammaton as well as the number of characters in the English Alphabet. We separated our alphabet in two creating 13 letters each to find their appropriate numbers. The number 13 is going to be very important in understanding just what calendar Jachin and Boaz are encoding. If we multiply the numbers of Jachin (4x1x3x6x5x1 =360) and multiply the numbers of Boaz (2x2x1x1 = 4) and then add the resulting numbers together, we discover the most revealing number of **364**, just one day short of our solar year. The missing day is represented by Christmas, or the day that the sun rises one degree on the horizon and starts the new year and the cycle of life over once again.

13 months with 28 days each (13 x 28 = 364) gives us a perfect calendar with every day being the same date and day as the previous year, a feature amiss in our current calendrical system. The celebration of Christmas would therefore not be counted on the calendar and would become a "day out of time". There are traditionally 12 houses of the Zodiac, known as our horoscope (horoscope derived from the words *Horus*, the Egyptian Sun God and *scope* meaning "space for movement") and each house is assigned particular periods spanning the 12 months. O*phiucus*, a constellation known as "the serpent holder" was recognized by the Greeks and quite possibly was used as a sign to directly correlate a 13 month calendar system to a 13 house Zodiac. Where else do we find this 364 day, 13 month calendar?

Playing cards have four suits, Diamonds, Spades, Hearts and Clubs, each consisting of 13 cards (Ace, 2, 3, 4, 5, 6, 7, 8, 9, 10, Jack, Queen and King). If we give numerical values to the Ace =1, Jack =11, Queen =12 and King =13, we find the sum of each suit to be 91. 1+2+3+4+5+6+7+ 8+9+10+11+12+13=**91**. If there are 4 suits we therefore have **91 x 4 = 364** with one Joker representing the "one day out of time" and the other representing the leap year. There are 52 cards in a deck which represent the 52 weeks in a year (4 weeks per month with a 13 month calendar 4 x 13 = 52).

Chichen Itza, a once thriving Mayan city located in the Yucatan Peninsula of Mexico, is said to be at least 1,500 years old. In Chichen Itza sits a nine level pyramid with 4 staircases of 91 steps each leading to its observatory, or temple, at the top. **91 x 4 = 364**, with the temple and star-obversatory representing the "one day out of time" (though they most likely imbedded this day within larger cycles of the heavens).

Stonehenge also imbeds the 13 month, 28 day calendar. There are 56 Aubrey holes, with each hole representing one day. 56/2 = 28. (See page 36 for a diagram) Therefore one rotation through the Aubrey Holes would equal 2 months of 28 days each. With the application of mirroring, and adding a decimal place, 56 now becomes 6.5. **6.5 x 56 = 364**. 6.5 rotations through the Aubrey Holes would equal a total of 13 months for one complete year with one day being "out of time". A leap year occurs every 4 years, where we have to add an entire day to our calendar to account for the extra 6 hours added to our solar year (365.24 - the .24 being just short of 6 hours). 4 years x 6.5 rotations through the Aubrey Holes would equal 26. 6.5 x 4 = 26. We know the importance of 26 as seen in the Hebraic Tetragrammaton summing to 26, as well as 26 being the number of letters in the English Alphabet.

The 364 day calendrical system was used by many different cultures from many different parts of the world and encoded in stone, game and mythology. Why have we abandoned this easy-to-use system and instead opted for a messy, 12 month, odd-numbered system? The ancients left us enough clues to help us map our place in cosmos, if for whatever reason, we may one day lose our place amongst the stars.

THE CASE FOR ASTROLOGY

Astrology is an ancient science that was practiced by numerous cultures around the world. Astrology was the firmly held belief that there is a direct relationship between astronomical phenomena and events that occur here on Earth. The human soul was considered intimately linked to the motions of the heavens above. Star and planet worship and the anthropomorphism of these heavenly bodies was of great importance to our ancestors. These Gods grace cathedrals and temples worldwide. Modern science sees astrology as a foolish, speculative and interpretive science and it is easy to see why when one reads the horoscope of many local papers. Is astrology a mere psuedo-science or have we simply lost the keys to the doorway of this knowledge? Did our ancestors lose their minds or have we forgotten how to use ours?

Zodiac literally translates to "cycle of life". The Zodiac, as seen below, is the 12 constellations, or houses, that the sun passes through in its 25,920 year cycle. Each age consists of 2,160 years with each age assigned one of the four basic alchemical elements: Earth, Water, Fire and Air.

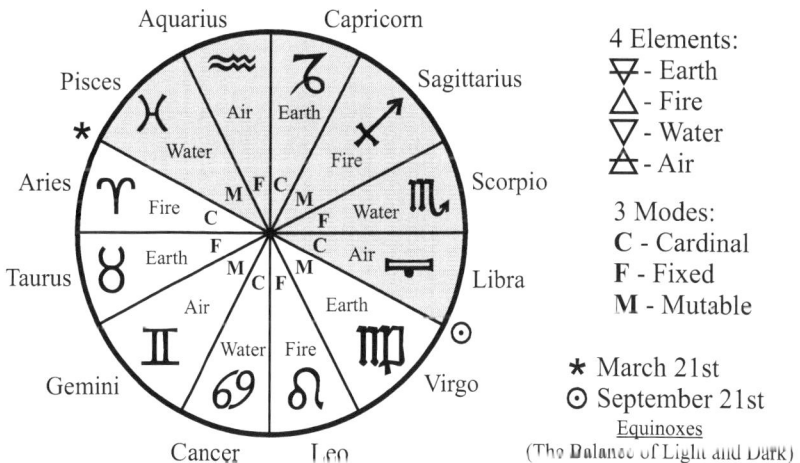

4 Elements:
▽ - Earth
△ - Fire
▽ - Water
△ - Air

3 Modes:
C - Cardinal
F - Fixed
M - Mutable

∗ March 21st
☉ September 21st
Equinoxes
(The Balance of Light and Dark)

The Zodiac has been called the Wheel of Fortune, the Wheel of Fate and the Wheel of Karma. Navigating through the zodiac's varying cycle is the quest of the hero. Getting off the wheel and into its center is his goal.

There are three modes, or qualities, that are used in Astrology termed Cardinal, Fixed and Mutable. *Cardinal* signs are energetic and dynamic, *Fixed* signs have persistence, perseverance and stability while *Mutable* signs are flexible and adaptable. These three qualities represent the movement and pace of the rising and falling of a singular turn on the Great Wheel in the sky.

The numerical equivalents of these three modes is most interesting.

CARDINAL   FIXED   MUTABLE
3 1 5 45 1 1 2 = **22**   6 5 3 5 4 = **23**   1 6 71 2 2 5 = **24**

Notice the progression from 22 to 23 to 24. Added together they equal **69**. There is another very interesting place we can find this number and that is in the heart of the alchemical process.

In alchemy there are three phases of trans-substantiation, or the process the self undergoes on the path to finding his true nature. These three phases are called the Nigredo, the Albedo and the Rubedo. Simply put, the Nigredo was the darkness of the ignorant animal man, the Albedo the illumination of truth and the Rubedo the ascent of whole spirit. The true meaning of the Rubedo has been kept secret for many years but we can get a glimpse of its glory within the words of the great Hermes in the Corpus Hermeticum:

"Ascend above any height, descend further than any depth; receive all sensory impressions of the created: water, fire, dryness, wetness. Think that you are present everywhere: in the sea, on earth and in the heaven; think that you were never born and that you are still in the embryonic state: young and old, dead and in the hereafter. Understand everything at the same time: time, place, things: quality and quantity."

The numerical equivalents of the three stages of Alchemy when added together equal **69**, the very same number as our three modes of astrology.

NIGREDO   ALBEDO   RUBEDO
1 5 7 55 4 2 = **29**   1 2 2 5 4 2 = **16**   5 6 2 5 4 2 = **24**

Where else do we find the number **69**?

This is the sign for Cancer. When the Sun enters the sign of Cancer during its travels through our skies this signifies the first day of Summer. The sun is at its highest point in the sky which represents the illumination of the self at its highest degree of spiritual awakening. It is the point when the light of the world is closest to Heaven. The science of astrology is the art of mapping the stars above within the motions of the self. The ancient Hermetic scholars understood that they were one and the same. The modes of astrology were akin to the phases of alchemy. It is most interesting that "Rubedo" and "Mutable" both equal 24 and Summer equals 24 as well. The red blood of the body becomes *mutable,* or mutated, into the glory of the pure light of the summer sun.

The equinoxes, March 21st and September 21st on our current calendars, are very special days. These two days mark the point in our solar year when both light and dark are equals or the point when day and night are of equal lengths. This swirling balance of light and dark is seen expressed in the Yin Yang symbol, yet another 6 and 9 nested with each other.

The Hermetic and alchemical wisdom spoke of the Alchemical Marriage, which was the unification of the opposites within the self (a concept we will go into further later in this text). The 6 and 9 represent the Yin and Yang, or duality, within the material world. To reach the stage of the Rubedo, the alchemist would have to merge these opposites into a complete whole. He would need to understand that he indeed was the entire wheel itself and therefore he could place himself on the center, or axle, and off the Wheel of Fortune and Fate. The axis is his throne to which he could watch over his entire kingdom. The alchemist understood that his own mind, his "Dome" was the entire universe and that he himself was KING of that DOMe. This ultimate truth was expressed in the Kybalion in the phrase "ALL is MIND."

THE TEMPLE OF MAN

The alchemist who held the philosopher's stone, or the mystic who sat on the throne of the Merkabah were in full realization that the entire Milky Way galaxy is in fact a reflection of the temple of man. The stars above our heads and the neurons in our heads are but reflections of each other. The human body is a mirror of the body of the universe. This is where we get the phrase "Man was made in the image of God."

The children's song "Twinkle, Twinkle Little Star" begs the listener to ponder on the nature of stars.

"Twinkle, twinkle little star. *How I wonder what you are!*"

The stars above represent the light of spirit within you. *Spirit* in Latin means "To breathe". To breathe is to speak and to speak is to sing. It is no coincidence that "Twinkle Twinkle Little Star" is set to the tune of the "Alphabet Song".

"As above, so below" gains a whole new meaning if one understands that the cycles of the Heavens above and the cycles here on Earth are but one motion of what the Kybalion calls, THE ALL. The UNIverse. The waters *below* here on Earth and the waters *above* in Heaven are but infinite reflections of each other. Place a mirror next to another mirror and what you will see is a miniature version of the entire universe. These mirrors present us with the idea of infinity, though, in all reality, they are merely reflecting each other's image. The human body is a divine, geometric, perfectly crafted vessel designed to navigate the spinning mirrors of these eternal counterparts existing as one. And with the power of sound, we have the ability to sing our way to the gates of our very own Heaven.

Alan Watts, a 20th century writer, lecturer and philosopher, once spoke that if one walked into an Ashram in India and proclaimed "I am God!", the yogis would say, "Congratulations, it's about time you found out." and if one walked into a Catholic Church and proclaimed the same, he'd be thrown from the chapel steps. The phrase "The Kingdom of God is within you" is actually telling you this to be fact. *You are God*. God and his kingdom resides *inside of you*. The Heavens above your head are inside of you. This is the PRESENT of God.

Below is an illustration of a man with the twelve constellations of the zodiac pointing to various parts of his body. Aries the Lamb is his head, Taurus the Bull is his neck, Gemini the Twins are his arms, Cancer the Crab is his chest, Leo the Lion is his heart (and kidneys), Virgo the Virgin is his stomach, Libra the Liberty is his hips, Scorpio the Scorpion is his phallus, Sagittarius the Archer is his thighs, Capricorn the Sea Goat is his knees, Aquarius the Water Bearer is his shins and Pisces the two fish are his feet. The twelve constellations represent the physiological, anatomical and spiritual makeup of the human being. This Twelve Ring Circus revolves right above our heads every single night in a retrograde motion (though they certainly appear fixed within our lifetimes). This motion represents the decay of all matter in the great movement of THE ALL. The journey we take through our lives and the journey the Earth and our solar system takes round the galaxy are but reflections of each other. They are one and the same. Notice the lamb, or Aries, is at the head of the individual. Jesus Christ being the "Lamb of God" and the Greek Lambda celebrated by the Pythagoreans are precise references to this constellation and its placement in the cosmic makeup of man.

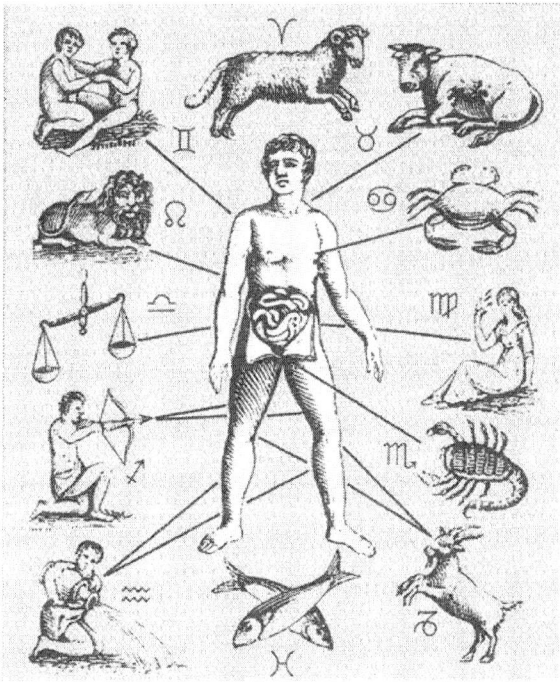

46

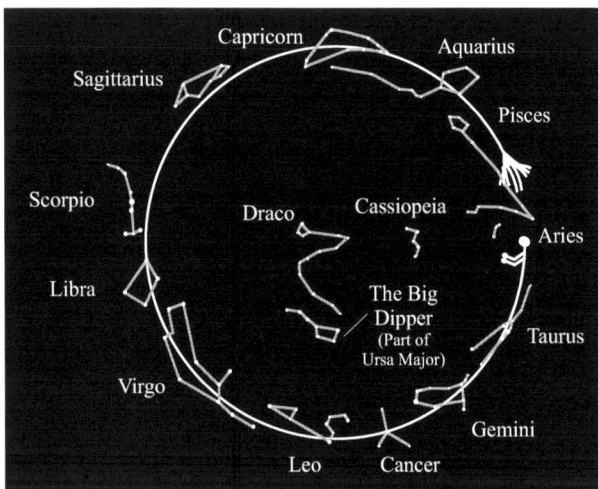

Above is a chart of the twelve constellations of the Zodiac. When the man from the Lakota sand painting (shown again below) is placed upon the circle of our Zodiac we can find a congruence with the illustration on the previous page. Aries the Lamb is the head of the Great Wheel of Life, its circumference being the human body resolving at the feet of the constellation Pisces. The Big Dipper, one of the most prominent constellations in the sky points to the tail of the constellation Draco. Draco is Latin for "Dragon". We will see the power of this Dragon, or serpent, one that forever rotates around our bodily center, later in this text. Cassiopeia, a motherly constellation forms an "M" also inside our bodily center. Mother is where we derive the word "matter". The English Alphabet can be symbolized by the letter "M".

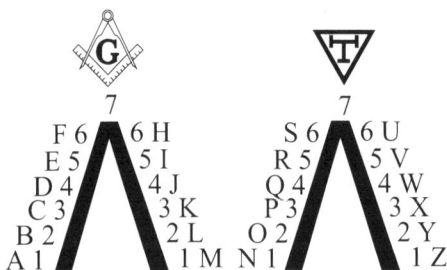

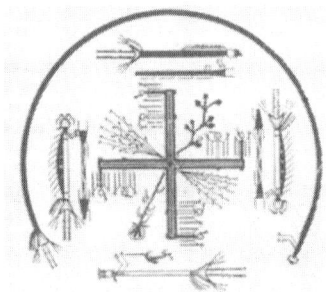

M - 26 Letters of the Alphabet

The "M" of Cassiopeia representing the 26 letters in the English Alphabet correlates to the constellation "Scorpio", which is itself an "M" and sums to **26**. "Mother", "Center", "Torus" (a geometric form we will explore in just a bit) and "Black Hole" all sum to **26** as well.

SCORPIO   MOTHER   CENTER
6 3 2 5 352 = **26**   1 27 65 5 = **26**   3 5 1 75 5 = **26**

TORUS   BLACK HOLE
72 5 66 = **26**   2 21 33 6 2 25 = **26**

Scorpio was the constellation on the cosmological makeup of man that represented the penis, or the vagina on a female, which are the regenerative members of the human body . Not coincidentally, the stinger of the Scorpion points to the center of our galaxy. Sagittarius, or the archer, has his bow drawn and arrow pointing to the center of our galaxy as well.

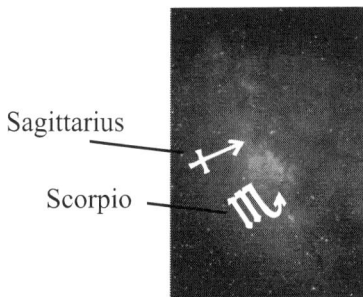

Sagittarius

Scorpio

The human body is a perfect mirror of itself. Your left eye is a mirror of your right eye, your left foot a mirror of your right foot, your left hand a mirror of your right hand, etc. There are two glaring exceptions to this rule though - one's navel and one's regenerative member - both of which happen to be very important in helping to bring new life into the world. The navel, in the center of one's stomach (noted by the constellation Virgo the Virgin) is the where the umbilical chord is attached, feeding the child growing inside the mother's womb. Scoprio is, of course, our sexual organs. Scorpio is also known as the "root" chakra in the ancient practice of Kundalini. It is here where all life begins. The Yin and Yang of the penis and vagina represent the two aspects of one universal motion. The penis gives and the vagina receives, only to then give a new child to the world. This physiological event is seen in the world of physics as well through Centripetal (toward the center) and Centrifugal (outward from center) forces. These principal opposites trade places at the vortex, or very center, of our galaxy.

In our Galactic Center exists what is known as a "Black Hole". A "Black Hole" is a region of space time where gravity prevents anything, including light, from escaping. Our galaxy is a torus, or shaped like a donut (as shown below). A torus is a self-regenerating system. The torus allows a vortex of energy to form which bends back along itself and re-enters itself, thus, continually renewing and influencing itself. The symbol for *Taurus* is a broken circle or bulls horns ♉ and is a reference to this universal shape since the torus itself is "broken" in its center. The Lakota symbol for "As above, so below" references this torus shape as well.

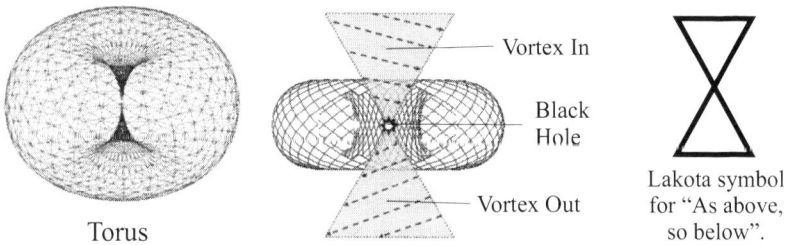

Torus

Vortex In

Black Hole

Vortex Out

Lakota symbol for "As above, so below".

The ancient symbol of the Flower of Life, created from 64 spheres, creates a torus as well when brought out to three dimensions. This holy geometric symbol is seen underfoot of a fierce lion in China as shown below.

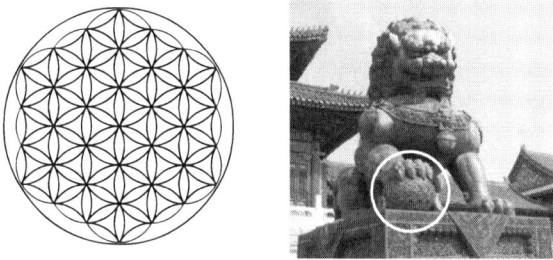

Taurus on the cosmological makeup of man was the neck. This is the part of the body upon on which the *dome of mind* sits.

Phonetically, Taurus can be spelled in three distinct ways.

TAURUS	TORUS	TORE US
♉	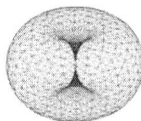	♉

Taurus the bull was often seen with a sphere or egg nestled between his horns (as seen below). This egg represents the primordial egg of our Universe (a concept we will explore in depth later). The symbol under the pronunciation of "Tore Us" is the Egyptian symbol for the cutting of this primordial egg, known by the term the "Primordial Scission". The word "Scissors" is derived from *scission* and notice the scissors right below the cosmic egg. "Tore us" represents man's fall from the Garden of Eden, "Torus" represents the universe's shape and "Taurus" represents the man who is "bull-headed" or strong enough to carry the *dome of mind* and the *high wisdom of the stars*.

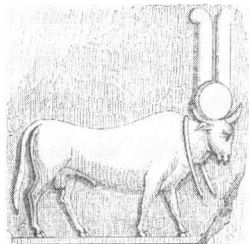

MERCURY

Hermes was akin to the god Mercury, or Mercurius, in Roman mythology. Mercury is the planet that is closets to our Sun which represents his illumination. Hermes completed the alchemical work, merging his opposites, unifying with THE ALL and recognizing his own mind was the mind of the Universe. The symbol for Mercury / Hermes is shown above. This symbol encodes "squaring the circle" with the cross and the circle, the cracking of the primordial egg of the Universe, the horns of Taurus the Bull and it also represents he who is closets to luminescence of the Sun. Hermes or Mercury was the man who understood that the Sun and the Galactic Center were but one and the same, both existing within the cosmic body of man himself. Hermes was *open-minded* enough to understand that he, in fact, was at the center of the vortex.

The numerical equivalents of the twelve houses of the Zodiac are listed below.

AQUARIUS   CAPRICORN   SAGITTARIUS   SCORPIO
1 4 6 1 5 5 6 6 = 34   3 1 3 5 5 3 2 5 1 = 28   6 1 7 5 7 7 1 5 5 6 6 = 56   6 3 2 5 3 5 2 = 26

LIBRA   VIRGO   LEO   CANCER   GEMINI
2 5 2 5 1 = 15   5 5 5 7 2 = 24   2 5 2 = 9   3 1 1 3 5 5 = 18   7 5 1 5 1 5 = 24

TAURUS   ARIES   PISCES
7 1 6 5 6 6 = 31   1 5 5 5 6 = 22   3 5 6 3 5 6 = 28

If we add up the sums to each of our twelve houses it equals **315**. (34 + 28 + 5 6+ 26 +15 + 24 + 9 + 18 + 24 + 31 + 22 + 28 = **315**) If we apply one of the cardinal rules of Gematria, "Coming up one short/extra" we can *subtract* "one" from that number and once again find the holy digits of Pi. **315** - 1 = 314, or **3.14**.

If we apply Decimal Parity to the products of our 12 houses of the Zodiac (Aquarius = 7, Capricorn = 1, Sagittarius = 2, Scorpio = 8, Libra = 6, Virgo = 6, Leo = 9, Cancer = 9, Gemini = 6, Taurus = 4, Aries = 4 and Pisces = 1) and add these up, we obtain the number **63**. The 33rd and highest degree of Freemasonry is the "Inspector General" and it equals **63**.

INSPECTOR GENERAL
5 1 6 3 5 3 7 2 5 7 5 1 5 5 1 2 = **63**

If we "come up one short" we can *add* "one" and yield the number **64**. 64 being once again, the number of codons that make up human DNA. It would seem that the number for the genetic instructions that make up human beings is esoterically and mathematically encoded in the heavens above.

If we reduce the number **63** down to its decimal parity equivalent, or **9** (6 + 3 = 9) and divide **315** by **9**, we yield the number **35**. (315 / 9 = 35) "Pi" in our cipher finds us the numbers **3** and **5**. We will revisit this 3 and 5, and its relationship to enlightenment, later in this text.

If we add the numerical equivalent of our 12 houses, **315,** and divide that total by the decimal parity equivalent addition of our twelve houses, or **63**, we yield the most interesting number **5**. 315 / 63 = **5**. Five, or Phi is a number that is most associated with man. MAN, or *mankind* being the *sons* and daughters of God.

51

If we "come up one short" and add 1 to our 315, we get the number 316. John 3:16 is one of the most often quoted verses in the Bible.

John **3:16**; For God so loved the world, that he gave his *only begotten Son*, that whosoever believeth in him should not perish, but have everlasting life."

We will see the power of this "only begotten son" and how it is a reflection of the power of spirit within you embedded in the holy name of Jesus Christ in just a bit. But first, let's first find the cross of Christ present in our very skies.

The current calendrical dates assigned to the Zodiac and their corresponding elements and modes are listed below.

♈	**Aries**: Cardinal Fire March 21 - April 20	**Libra**: Cardinal Air September 23 - October 22	♎
♉	**Taurus**: Fixed Earth April 21 - May 21	**Scorpio**: Fixed Water October 23 - November 21	♏
♊	**Gemini**: Mutable Air May 22 - June 21	**Sagittarius**: Mutable Fire November 22 - December 21	♐
♋	**Cancer**: Cardinal Water June 22 - July 22	**Capricorn**: Cardinal Earth December 22 - January 20	♑
♌	**Leo**: Fixed Fire July 23 - August 23	**Aquarius**: Fixed Air January 21 - February 19	♒
♍	**Virgo**: Mutable Earth August 24 - September 22	**Pisces**: Mutable Water February 20 - March 20	♓

THE GREAT CROSS IN THE SKY

The cross is one of the most widely known and venerated symbols used throughout the ages. Pagans, druids, Christians and indigenous peoples across the world have used this symbol as representative of their particular gods or deities. Though the cross has many symbolic meanings, its deepest significance lies in its use in mapping the Heavens above our heads. Following and mapping the path of the sun and the stars was considered one of most holy sciences. Doing so helped align oneself to the cycles of the cosmos and therefore, in turn helped *align oneself*. We know of Jesus Christ being "nailed to the cross", which proceeded his subsequent death and then resurrection. This death and resurrection is an allegory used in many cultures from the Zoroastrian Mithras to the Greek Dionysus to the Hiram Abiff legend told by the Freemasons. Jesus Christ was the "Son" of God. If we follow our allegorical rules, we understand that "Son" becomes the "Sun" in our sky, his death and resurrection the rebirth of a cycle and Jesus being "nailed to the cross" recognized as nothing more than the Sun following a universal pattern.

On Dec. 22
The Sun stops moving South
and "dies" on the Cross
(Under the Southern Crux
constellation)

It is dead for 3 days
Dec 22, 23 & 24

Only to rise again Dec 25th
The Sun moves
1 degree North
and the Cycle
of Life starts again.

Since the cross is one of the most holy of symbols, the numerical equivalent of "cross" should therefore be as holy as the as symbol itself.

CROSS
3 5 2 6 6 = **22**

5 Points
+ 2 Lines
―――――――
7 Pieces

"Cross" sums to 22. The cross was constructed by the metaphorical 7 days of creation and therefore 22/7 = 3.142, or a rough approximation of Pi. There are also 5 points and two intersecting lines on the cross making a total of 7 pieces. 22 / 7 Pieces = 3.142. If we multiply the numbers of "Cross" (3x5x2x6x6) we end up with the number 1,080, which is the radius of the Moon in miles as well as our Holy number 108 x 10.

There are three great crosses that occur in our sky. One is the cross created by our solstices and equinoxes and our four seasons; another is known as the galactic cross which is made by the equator of our galaxy and the ecliptic of our solar system; the final cross is made by the sun rising and setting on the horizon. Let's first take a look at the cross that is made every single day by the sun, the sunrise, the sunset and where this all occurs, the horizon.

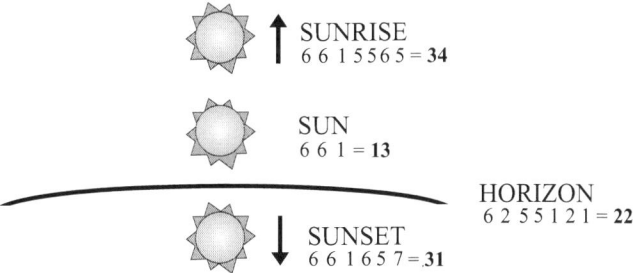

SUNRISE
6 6 1 5 56 5 = **34**

SUN
6 6 1 = **13**

HORIZON
6 2 55 1 2 1 = **22**

SUNSET
6 6 1 65 7 = **31**

If we add up sunrise, sun, horizon and sunset, the sum equals **100** (34+13+31+22 = **100**, which is nothing more than 10, representing our base 10 system, squared (10x10 = 100). Horizon equals 22 and there are 7 letters in horizon, which can once again get us an approximation of Pi, 22/7 = 3.142

The solstices and equinoxes can also help us obtain the number **100** if we add the numerical equivalents of our four seasons: Winter (27), Spring (27), Summer (24) and Autumn (22). (27+27+24+22 = **100**)

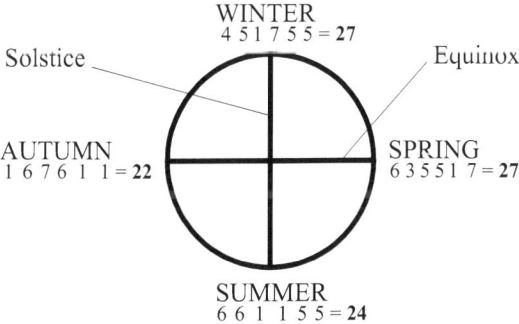

WINTER
4 51 7 5 5 = **27**

Solstice

Equinox

AUTUMN
1 6 76 1 1 = **22**

SPRING
6 3 55 1 7 = **27**

SUMMER
6 6 1 1 5 5 = **24**

The last great cross we will look at is the galactic cross made by the equator of our galaxy and the ecliptic of our solar system. Our solar system revolves around the center of our galaxy at a 60 degree angle as shown below.

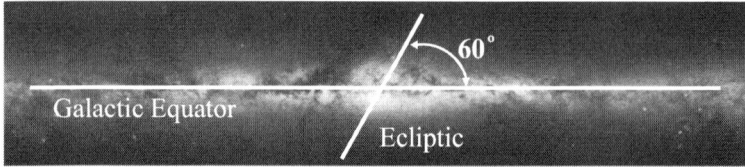

Galactic Equator

60°

Ecliptic

This Great Cross was signified by four constellations; the Galactic Equator by Taurus and Scorpio and the Ecliptic by Leo and Aquarius. If we add the numerical equivalents of these four fixed signs, we obtain, once again, the number **100**. $(34 + 26 + 31 + 9 = 100)$

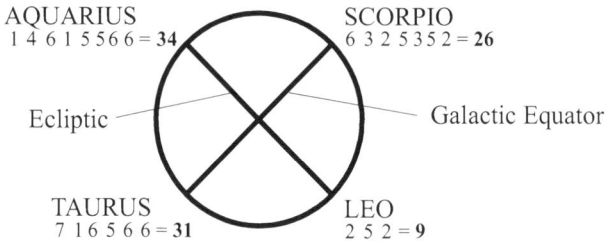

AQUARIUS
1 4 6 1 5 5 6 6 = **34**

SCORPIO
6 3 2 5 3 5 2 = **26**

Ecliptic

Galactic Equator

TAURUS
7 1 6 5 6 6 = **31**

LEO
2 5 2 = **9**

Matthew 5:13 says, "Ye are the salt of the earth: but if the salt have lost his savior, where with shall it be salted?". What is this "salt" Matthew speaks of? If we take the first letters of our four fixed signs, it we find our answer:

Scorpio   **A**quarius   **L**eo   **T**aurus

S.A.L.T. This is also most likely where the term "ATLAS" is derived.

Could all of these crosses adding up to 100 be just a simple coincidence?

In Islam, it is said that there are 99 names of Allah. Why 99? Why not an even 100? It would seem that Islam has left out 1 very important holy name of God. In actuality, they didn't *leave out* anything at all, that is of course if you understand that you have to include your own name on that list.

55

THE FOUR HORSEMEN

The Galactic Cross was one of the most venerated concepts in Christian and pagan mythology and scripture. The four signs of the zodiac referenced the ecliptic of our solar system and the galactic equator. These "Four Horsemen" of the apocalypse or our four fixed points were mythologized as a Man, a Lion, a Bull and an Eagle or Scorpion. The Man was the constellation Aquarius the Water Bearer, the Lion was Leo, the Bull was Taurus and the Eagle, or the Scorpion, was Scorpio. The eagle, or phoenix, has been a symbol that has been used by alchemists and Freemasons for ages. The phoenix was the bird that would rise up from the ashes of destruction. The eagle would fly to the highest of heavens and the scorpion would point the way.

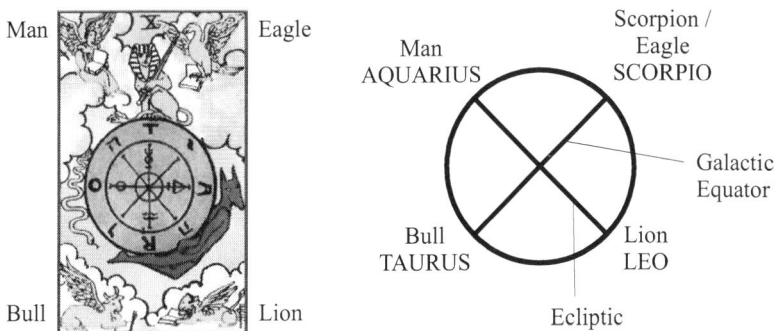

Apocalypse literally means "uncovering" or "unveiling" and these four points in the sky, aligned at a certain time period in our great cycle of the Precession of the Equinoxes would signify a point of "uncovering" or "unveiling" of the hidden knowledge of the nature of existence. The Seasonal Cross and Galactic Cross are often symbolized together *simply* by two crosses, tilted **45** degrees from each other, creating **8** parts. We will see the power of this ***Eightfold Way*** a bit later.

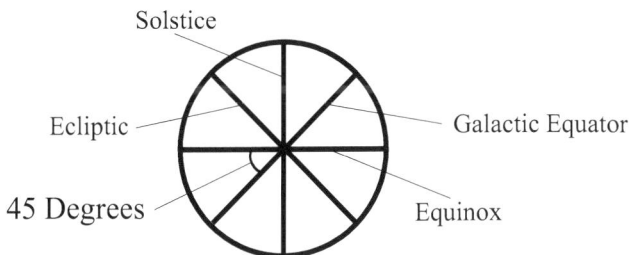

The "Four Horsemen" of the apocalypse also equals the number **45** if we add the sum of the four classic fixed points: Man, Eagle, Lion and Bull. "And the first beast was like a lion, and the second beast like a calf, and the third beast had a face as a man, and the fourth beast was like a flying eagle." - Revelation 4:7. Both "calf" and "bull" equal 12.

MAN   EAGLE   LION   BULL
1 1 1   5 1 7 2 5   2 5 2 1   2 6 2 2 = **45**

Scripture says that "The kingdom of God is within you." (Luke 17:21) and the philosophers of old will tell you of a God whose "circumference is nowhere and center everywhere". The **45** degree sections created by our galactic and seasonal crosses become our *arcs* and our *angles*. The *Arc* that Noah sailed on to withstand the great deluge of the apocalypse was nothing more than Noah understanding this deep-rooted knowledge. The *Arc* of the Covenant, in one metaphorical sense, could come to mean that our *covenant* with God is recognizing and accepting the fact that the Earth will be destroyed and a new civilization will rise anew. The cyclic crosses above our heads remind us of this absolute in nature. Everything is a cycle. Growth and decay, birth and death, past and future are but one movement upon the eternal wheel of creation. This **45** degree angle, creating our arc, is nothing more than our archangel, guiding us to the gates of the heaven within oneself. The true *philosopher* will realize what *scripture* was truly trying to say.

PHILOSOPHER   SCRIPTURE
3 6 52 2 6 2 3 6 5 5 = **45**   6 3 55 3 7 6 5 5 = **45**

45 is also an important number because it is encoded in the divine 9 of our number line. 1+2+3+4+5+6+7+8+9 = **45**. 45, using Pythagorean addition also equals 9 (4 + 5 = **9).** In mathematics there is a function known as casting out nines which, when used with Pythagorean addition, allows a person to check their arithmetic with ease. (Example: **4** +**9** = 13 and 1 + 3 = **4** therefore **4** = 4). The 9 was known as the serpent, an idea we will cover later in this text, and casting out this 9 or this serpent was akin to the metaphor of casting out the demon inside onself. It was the mathematical equivalent of snake charming.

Last, but certainly not least, "Horseman" equals 27. If there were four of these men they combined would equal, once again, our Holy 108. 4 x 27 (Horseman) − **108**.

THE NEWS OF THE WORLD

Mankind orients himself with four cardinal directions; North, East, West and South. We derive the word "NEWS" from these four points on the *compass*. The journey through life could indeed be deemed the "*News* that *com*es to *pass*."

Throughout the year, our Earth spins on its axis and around the sun, creating day and night and the four seasons: Winter, Spring, Summer and Autumn. Autumn is sometimes called Fall (no doubt a reference to the "fall" of man since this is the season prior to Winter). Fall and Autumn do not have the same numerical equivalent. "Fall" sums to 11 and "Autumn" sums to 22. Without the 22 of Autumn, our seasonal cross will not equal **100**. We find ourselves at a crossroads. Or do we?

WINTER	SPRING	SUMMER	FALL
4 5 1 7 5 5 = **27**	6 3 5 5 1 7 = **27**	6 6 1 1 5 5 = **24**	6 1 2 2 = **11**

The sum of the numerical equivalents of the four seasons, using fall, equals **89**. 89 is both a prime and Fibonacci number.

The numerical equivalents of NEWS sum to **89** as well.

NORTH	EAST	WEST	SOUTH
1 2 5 7 6 = **21**	5 1 6 7 = **19**	4 5 6 7 = **22**	6 2 6 7 6 = **27**

 The four cardinal directions have a direct correspondence to the four seasons our of solar year.

If we take the decimal parity or Pythagorean addition equivalents of the first three letters of NEWS or *NEW!*, we once again find the Holy ratio of Pi.

NORTH	EAST	WEST
1 2 5 7 6 = **21**	5 1 6 7 = **19**	4 5 6 7 = **22**
2 + 1 =	1+9=10 (1 + 0) =	2 + 2 =
3	**1**	**4**

3 . 1 4

The *compass* is of course the tool we use to find that holy ratio of Pi. The simple drawing of a circle with our compass encapsulates the entire motion of the Earth and the self within the continuous cycles of our spinning universe.

PHI AND PHILOS

The term philosophy comes to us from the most famous of all Greek mathematicians and mystics, Pythagoras. Philosophy is the study and science of the fundamental questions of existence, consciousness, reason and language. As implied by the word itself, the core of this science was done using numbers. The "Phi" and "Phee" of **PHI**loso**PHEE** are direct references to the ratio of Phi and its counterpart, Phee, and evidence that in order to get to the heart of the matter of all things, one needs to start with the study of numbers. Pythagoras' most famous phrase was "All is number," and Plato informed us that "Numbers are the highest degree of knowledge. It is knowledge itself." "Philos" was a term used by the Greeks that meant "loving brethren". It was a term shared by a society that understood that each and every single human being was of divine nature and had the love of the great spirit within them. The Greeks celebrated a high culture, basking in the glory of the arts and sciences. They recognized the sacredness of the world they inherited and memorialized it in their mythologies and architecture.

The sum of the numerical equivalent of Phi equals 14, a number we will explore in depth further in this text but for now, let's concentrate on the three numbers of "Phi" and the sum of the title of "Philos".

PHI   PHILOS
365   365226 = **24**

It should immediately jump out at you that Phi actually encodes the number of days our Earth revolves around the Sun - **365** days a year. The sum of Philos equals 24, or the number of hours in one Earth day. The Egyptians were supposedly the first to accurately calculate the number of days in the solar year, or **365.24** days. Putting the letters of "Phi" along with the addition of "Philos" together yields us this number **365.24**. The Egyptians mapped our solar year by mapping another prominent star in the sky, Sirius. Sirius, as previously noted, sums to 33, or the highest degree of Freemasonic ascension. The heliacal rising (or rising with the sun) of Sirius signified the flooding of the Nile River. This annual event allowed the Egyptians to map time here on Earth to a clock in the heavens with relative ease. Phi was indeed important to the Egyptians for both the Great Pyramid of Giza as well as the Temple at Luxor incorporate into their architecture this magical ratio.

The multiplication of the individual letters of Philos results in the most interesting set of numbers:

Φ

PHI: 3 x 6 x 5 = **90**
There are 90 degrees in a right angle, 1/4 of 360 degrees

PHIL: 3 x 6 x 5 x 2 = **180**
180 degrees is exactly one half of a circle

PHILO: 3 x 6 x 5 x 2 x 2 = **360**
The number of degrees in a circle

PHILOS: 3 x 6 x 5 x 2 x 2 x 6 = **2,160**
2,160 is the number of years for one zodiacal age (splitting the Precession of the Equinoxes into the traditional 12 houses, 12 x 2,160 = 25,920 years). The diameter of the Moon is 2,160 miles.

Multiplying the sum of the multiplication of Philos, or 2,160, times the sum of the addition of Philos, or 24 yields us the number 51,840. This is exactly two Precessional periods of 25,920 years.

Phi is a phenomenon that is not only a mathematical ratio expressed all throughout the natural world, but one that is embedded in our speech, the movement of the stars above our heads and shows its face in the movement of our solar system. We speak its language and wear its ratio on the vehicles of flesh that we inhabit. It is the balancing point, or the "mean", that gives us *meaning* to this existence. Phi helps us understand that creation is perfect and ultimately through all of its complexities, at its heart, is really very simple. Though we may feel divided from one another and from our natural surroundings, Phi reminds us that the same *meaning* that grows a flower or a tree in your backyard is the same *meaning* that grows you. Its *meaning* connects all things. Philos, or "loving brethren" is not simply a kind title to address some one, but an actual statement about all of creation. Creation is your concomitant, your partner, your brother, and when you see its simplicity, you will understand that underlying all of its duality and seeming harshness lies a deep love that cannot be distinguished or destroyed. It is the love pouring forth from the mouth of God.

THE RIVER OF THE LORD

In Genesis we learn of the "waters" that separated Heaven and Earth and how the Spirit of God moved over these waters. Rivers and bodies of water have been important to countless religions, cultures and civilizations throughout time. No doubt rivers were important when it came to commerce, trade and as a source for food, but rivers and bodies of water also had a deeper symbolic significance. The river was the divine force that emanated from the heart of the supreme being. The "mouth" of the Lord uttering all of creation and the mouth of a river are linguistically identical and this is no coincidence. Baptismal rituals traditionally were performed in rivers or streams. The Nile River was a much venerated body of water by the Egyptians for not only did it amply provide for their civilization, but it also flows from the south to the north, a symbolic current heading towards the palace of the Heavens above. The Red Sea lying between Africa and Asia was so named not because it was red in color, but instead because it represented the blood that flows through the human body. It represents the river or body of water inside us, pumped by our heart, that gifts us with the magic of being.

Notice the numerical equivalent of the word river has a singular numerical flow.

RIVER
5 5 5 5 5

5 is once again, the number of the Golden Mean of Phi, the all-important ratio present throughout the natural world. It seems the river of the mouth of the lord allegorically not only gives us the waters of reflection, the fluidity of all things, but it also gives a mathematical ratio to which we grow into. "Revive" and "River" are both made up of continuos fives and this is no accident. The ratio of Phi is a constant in nature that brings us and all animate forms to life, in a cyclic fashion, from birth to death and back to birth again. In Genesis 2:10 - 2:11, the Bible speaks of a river that "went out of Eden to water the garden", which parted the Garden of Eden. This river was named "Pison" and was "that which encompasseth the whole land". The name **Pi**son is not arbitrary. Pi is of course the ratio of a circle's circumference to its diameter, one of the most powerful mathematical constants, and does in fact encompass the whole. The most important message, though, that Genesis prophetically reminds us is that in the land that this river encompasses, "*there is* gold". That gold being, of course, you.

If the river "Pison", is indeed a reference to the infinite, transcendental number of Pi, or 3.141, then we should find this river in the compass itself. The compass and square were most important to the alchemists. And of course, the compass and square make up the key insignia to the Freemasons. Jesus of Nazareth, before becoming "Christ", was a carpenter and no carpenter of old could do his work without these Freemasonic and alchemical tools. The numerical equivalents of compass and square are most revealing. Compass equals 22 and Square equals 27.

COMPASS   SQUARE
3 2 1 3 1 6 6 = **22**   6 4 6 1 5 5 = **27**

The first thing about "compass" that immediately stands out is that it sums to 22. If we are looking to find the river Pison, or that which "compasseth the whole" all we need to do is divide the numerical equivalent of Compass, by the number of letters in the name and we end up with a whole number approximation of Pi (22/7 = 3.142). We can also divide this 22 by the "G" in the center of the Freemasonic symbol, or the 7th letter of the alphabet and again, find our ratio of Pi.

The sum of "square" is just as revealing. If you page back to our cipher, you will notice that the prime numbers in our cipher - 2, 3, 5, 7, 5, 3, 2 - add up to 27 for each side of our alphabet and the 27 bones in each of your hands. In order to form an actual square, we would need *two squares* from the Freemasonic symbol, creating the Earthly square known by the sacred geometers to be the very bones in your two hands.

27 bones   27 bones

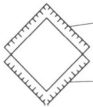

Square = 27 (left hand w/ 27 bones)

Square = 27 (right hand w/ 27 bones)

The compass and square symbolize the concepts of Heaven and Earth, the compass being Heaven and the Square being Earth. We can find the river connecting the two by taking the difference of Heaven and Earth. The multiplication of Compass equals 648 (3x2x1x3x1x6x6) and the multiplication of Square equals 3,600 (6x4x6x1x5x5). Earth, or the square, divided by Heaven, or the compass, yields us the nothing less than the Mouth of the "River" of the Lord; 3,600 / 648 = **5.5555...**

RIVER
5 5 5 5 5

62

THE 7 DAYS OF CREATION

The number 7 is the one number, out of all the other infinite numbers, that is the most holy, most revered and most celebrated. According to Genesis, creation itself was completed in seven days. Judaism, Islam, Hinduism, Ba'hai and Wiccan religions are all littered with references to this most esteemed number. Seven stars are easily recognizable in Ursa Major (or the Bigger Dipper, as it is commonly known today) and seven stars make up the Pleaides (sometimes known as the "Seven Sisters"). Snow White had her Seven Dwarfs and baseball has its 7th inning stretch. Why has there been such a focus on this magical number?

The alchemists frequently noted the seven visible heavenly bodies in our night sky (Saturn, Jupiter, Mars, Venus, Mercury, the Sun and the Moon). The sacred geometers deemed Heaven as 3 and Earth as 4 and therefore the merging of Heaven and Earth would equal 7. Man is said to suffer from seven deadly sins, there are seven days of the week, seven notes of the major scale (A, B, C, D, E, F, G), seven colors of the rainbow (Red, Orange, Yellow, Green, Blue, Indigo, Violet) and in the Endocrine system there are said to be seven chakras, or energy centers, in the human body. All vibratory phenomena, which of course includes sound and light, tends to completion in seven stages. We have been exploring the notion that the entire universe was created by an all encompassing sound and therefore, with vibration having a 7 fold nature, it would be easy to understand why the biblical creation story relies so heavily on the holy number 7. As we have previously discussed, there are six directions - Up /down, left / right, forward and reverse with *you* resting on the axis, or Sabbath, which combined finds us that holy number 7. Seven is a prime number, not only mathematically but also theologically.

Since seven is such a holy number, the numerical equivalent of seven should be holy as well. And once again, nothing is more *wholly* than the ratio of Pi.

SEVEN	MIRACLE
6 5 5 5 1 = **22**	1 5 5 1 3 2 5 = **22**

22 divided by "Seven" yields us Pi. 22 / SEVEN = 3.142. Understanding the power of seven also allows us to perform a "Miracle". "Miracle" equals 22 and there are seven letters in the word. 22 divided by 7 yields us once again, a close approximation of that miraculous, infinite, transcendental number of Pi.

Genesis exclaims "God said let there be light". The manifestation of sound and light seem to be the key in understanding creation. Human beings are constructed using 23 pairs of chromosomes. Let's take a closer look at the word we use to describe us as a species as well as the word we use to describe the make up of our genetic material.

*HUE*man *CHROMA*somes

The words hue and chroma are references to light and color. Hue, etym-ologically also means "a shouting" or "a calling, outcry". The very words we use to describe the entire human race seem to have their origin in color, sound and the 7-fold nature of vibration. The mythology of the world being created in 7 days is often dismissed by modern science but this mythological motif ceases to be so outlandish if we peer into the deeper meaning that it conceals. The seven branched menorah is a symbol that we have seen used on the Holy 108 as well as on our English Alphabet. This symbol has deep roots and speaks to the subconscious in ways we may just be beginning to understand.

The 360 degrees of a circle can be divided equally by our base ten system except for one number and that is, of course, 7. 360 divided by 7 gives us the number 51, a number we will explore in depth later, and a repeating string of the decimals 1, 4, 2, 8, 5 and 7. $360/7 = 51.\overline{428571}428571...$

If we draw a circle and put 9 numbers around it connecting the repeating decimals of the division of 360 by 7, we obtain the symbol known as the Enneagram. The Enneagram was a symbol celebrated by the alchemists and made popular by the philosopher G.I. Gurdieff and was deemed the "Symbol of Enlightenment".

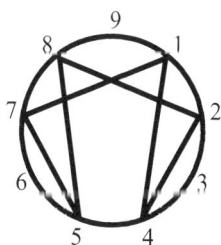

Connect
1, 4, 2, 8, 5, 7, 1
on the number dial
to find the Enneagram

$360/7 = 51.\overbrace{428571}...$

It seems that even the search for enlightenment itself is intimately conn-ected to that holy number seven.

THE VIRGIN MARRIED

Next to Jesus, the Virgin Mary, the mother of Christ, is probably the most adored character in the Christian lexicon. The miraculous feat of her giving birth to Jesus, the "Sun of God", after being impregnated by the Holy Spirit is a story that echoes the Egyptian story of Isis. Isis was impregnated by a golden phallus (a symbol that carries with it heavy mystical meaning) and gave birth to Horus, the Sun god of Egypt. Horus and Jesus are mythologically the same character and share many similar traits. Both of these stories encode, through anthropomorphism, a reflection of the story of creation. If we symbolize the first thing of creation as a circle (representing all or nothing), then in order to give birth to another circle, or a unit such as *one*, it would have to impregnate itself, or *double itself*. Since most all of creation needs a partner to make offspring, this initial impregnation had to be done by deific means. It had to be *miraculous*. The Virgin Mary was often signified by the symbol of the Vesica Piscis, or two circles overlapping on each other's centers. This symbol was also known as the almond or the "golden womb." Jesus Christ was often seen nestled inside the womb, or overlap, of these two circles (shown below). The two circles and womb make three shapes representing the Holy Trinity. Piscis and Isis are very similar phonetically and this is no accident. Also notice the **Pi** in the name of **Pi**scis as well as the "scis" signifying a scission or cutting open of the initial womb or circle of creation.

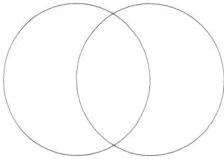

"Virgin" etymologically means "Unmarried". Using homonyms once again as our guide, the Virgin Mary can be translated to the "Unmarried Married". This presents one immediately with a paradox; How can something be married and unmarried at the same time? How can something be joined and disjointed simultaneously? How can a child be born of a virgin? The Holy Bible is riddled with paradoxes such as these and this was done intentionally (the Earth being created and yet "formless and void" is another prime example). Paradoxes and anomalies make the reader think beyond the scope of his or hers everyday conceptions. In order to understand the will and workings of God, one needed to transcend everyday mental constructs; one would need to dive head first into the realms of paradox.

The question "Can God make a rock so heavy that he himself could not lift it?" is not a question to prove that there is no God, but a question posed to initiate the common, animal man into the deep realms of philosophy and spiritual insight.

The paradoxical character of the "Unmarried Mary" has many symbolic connotations but the one we will focus on is one that is probably least often identified in the story of the Mary. Her impregnation is a symbolic represent-ation of the Unity of Opposites that exist within all beings. In order for her to become pregnant and give birth to the "Son of God", she would need an inter-nal male counterpart to help her conceive. Since Mary was said to have been impregnated by "The Holy Spirit", let's take a look at the words "Holy" and "Spirit" and their homonym counterparts:

WHOLLY   SPEAR IT

$$\Phi$$

As we discussed with the symbol of Phi, the line represents the male, or phallus, signified by the "Spear" in spirit and the circle represents the female, or vagina, in "Wholly".

The Holy Spirit itself carries within it the dual characteristics of both male and female. If we were to make these opposites unified again, we would need to marry them. The internal man would need to unite with the external female of Mary. The paradox of "Unmarried Married" would have to be nullified.

Carl Jung, one the great psychologists of the 20th century, introduced, through his study of alchemy, the concepts of the Anima and the Animus. Beyond the ego, in the deepest recesses of one's self, lay a polar reflection of the opposite sex. I.E. within every man lies a woman and within every woman lies a man. This concept was known in alchemy as the alchemical marriage or wedding. This marriage was almost invariably signified by either a single body with two heads, (one being a man and one a woman - see page 20) or simply by the Sun and Moon. This psychological marriage of the opposites within oneself was necessary to undergo in order to complete the great alchemical work. Marrying the opposites that existed within the soul man-ifested a wholeness of self and actualized the supreme being that was divided within.

The circle has always represented Heaven and is symbolic of the andro-gynous nature of the first thing. This *herma*phroditic first cause is mytholo-gized in the name of *Hermes* Trismegistus, the great Egyptian philosopher.

Numerically, Virgin Mary is very interesting.

VIRGIN MARY
5 5 5 7 5 1 1 1 5 2 = **37**

Virgin Mary sums to 37. 3 plus 7 equals 10, which is a number of com-pletion noted by the ten fingers of our hands and our base ten system. The 3 signifies the Holy Trinity and 7, the number of days in which God took to create the world. The Holy Trinity being one supreme being is reflected in a single white light passing through a triadic glass prism and casting the refracted rays upon a screen in the seven colors of the spectrum - a simple light show that symbolizes all of creation. The Virgin Mary symbolizing the unification of the opposites of man and woman within the self can also be seen in one of the most popular games of the ages; Chess.

The two most powerful pieces on the board are the King and Queen. Virgin Mary equaled **37** and 3 x 7 = 21. 21 is the same numerical equivalent of the word "Queen" (46551). "King" (3517) has a numerical equivalent of 16. 21 + 16 equals **37**, our hermaphroditic number. In the game of chess, the key players are the King, the Queen and *you* - together representing the Holy Trinity. The father is the King, the Queen is the Holy Spirit and you are the "Son" or the "Son of God". If we utilize Pythagorean addition, Queen sums to 3 (21 being 2 + 1 = 3) and King sums to 7 (16 being 1 + 6 = 7) giving us, once again, the numbers 3 and 7. Chess, the Egyptian Hermes, the Virgin Mary, and as we will see in the following pages, Jesus Christ all encoded with-in their characterizations this psychological unity of opposites. The mystics of old understood that in order to win the game of life, one must marry the King and Queen within oneself. Wholeness could not be realized without it.

Music encodes the alchemical wedding as well. "Sharp" (or the "*Spear*") equals 21 and "Flat" (or the "*Wholly*") equals 16, combining to make **37**.

Even Stonehenge encodes this alchemical marriage. The "Altar Stone" in the center of the Sarsen Circle was the stone in which one would "Alter" his or her own ego. Altar sums to 16 and Stone sums to 21, once agin, equaling **37**.

THE LUNAR TICK

The number 37 shows its face in our night skies and is also encoded in the always feminine silvery Moon. A lunar month, or what is called a synodic month, is a time period of 29.5 days and is the cycle from new moon to full moon.

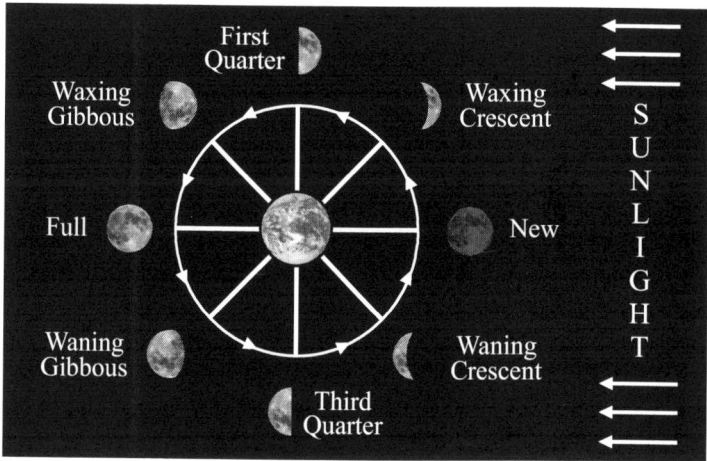

12 synodic months equals 354 days (12 x 29.5 = 354). There are twelve moons and a fraction in one year and therefore it would take three years, to make an extra moon or month. This would give us 36 months with the **37**th month being lunar / solar equilibrium. It is the calendrical shift between 3 and 4 years, or the difference between the sacred geometrical Heaven (3) and Earth (4). The **37**th month and the Virgin Marry equaling **37** point to the same phenomenon: the unification of opposites.

This roughly one third fraction in the Lunar Year can be found hiding in the 5, 12, 13 Pythagorean triangle. This triangle fits perfectly within the station stones at Stonehenge and was used to map the days of the week by the Aubrey Holes (see page 36). Solomon's Temple in Jerusalem was defined by its proportions. If we divide the opposite side of the Lunation Triangle, or the 5, between 2 and 3, this gives us the length for the line as **12.369**, or 12 and roughly a third. This *Silver Fraction* was determined to be the difference between 12 and 13. A pentagram drawn to a unit of 13 will also encode this fraction between the arms of the star. (Illustrations on the following page).

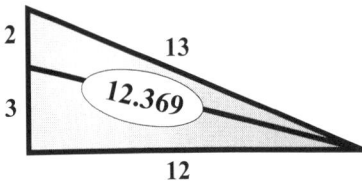

A "Perfect" 5, 12, 13 Pythagorean
Triangle

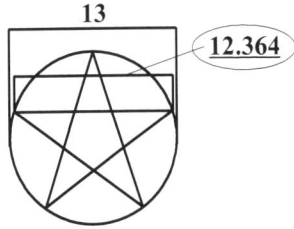

The Silver Fraction - The Difference between 12 & 13
One Lunation Period (29.53 days)

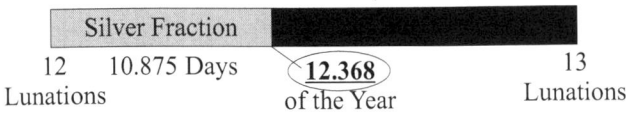

Silver Fraction	
12 10.875 Days 12.368	13
Lunations of the Year	Lunations

$$12.369 \times 29.53 = 365.25$$

The numerical equivalent of "Moon" is 6, representative of the 6 phases between new and full moons. Notice we split our alphabet at the "M" and "N", and Moon begins and ends with these two letters, leaving 2 letters between them, O and O. We can shed light on what happened in the first moments of our universe by uniting these two Os.

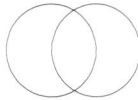

The Vesica Piscis is known as the golden womb of the universe and is akin to Isis and Mary. These two circles are but mirrors of each other. Water reflecting on water. We see this very reflection in the word MOON.

MOON
1 2 2 1

$$144 = 12^2 \mid 21^2 = 441$$

Notice the reflection of 12 in MO and 21 in ON. If we square these mirrored numbers (an idea we will explore in depth later, in the chapter titled "The Garden of Even", page 85) we yield yet another set of mirrored numbers, 144 / 441. This mirroring created the unified opposites that exist throughout the world and these opposites are most often symbolized with nothing more than a Sun and a Moon.

69

THE MONAD LISA

Leonardo Da Vinci is widely considered one of the most famous and significant figures in all of human history. He was a painter, sculptor, architect, musician, scientist, mathematician, engineer, inventor and anatomist. Leonardo, more so than any other figure, helped fuel the Italian Renaissance. Leonardo has many well known works such as *The Last Supper* and *The Vitruvian Man* but none is as well known as the *Mona Lisa*. Why has this rather small painting captivated the minds and hearts of generations of people? What is it about this woman that draws us in? What is that smirk on her face concealing?

It is well known that Leonardo modeled the Mona Lisa after the proportions of his own body and face. *The Mona Lisa* is not the portrait of a local Florentine woman but instead a portrait of the inner woman that existed within Leonardo. Within each human being lies a polar reflection of their external self. *The Mona Lisa* was painted to express what so many great minds before him knew; that man is internally divided and to understand the divine, one would need to merge those opposites.

"Mona" is undoubtedly a reference to the Moon or Luna as the moon is always associated with the female (women's premenstrual cycle is intimately connected to the synodic lunar cycle). Further, the Greek *Monad*, or symbol for wholeness added up to 361 in their gematria. The numerical equivalent of Mona Lisa sums to **19**.

MONA LISA
1 2 1 1 256 1 = **19**

The Greek Monad = 361
$\sqrt{361}$ = **19**

The square root of Monad, or 361, equals **19**. Leonardo understood that wholeness was achieved by merging the Sun "*Monad*" and Moon, "*Mona*".

JESUS CHRIST, THE "SUN" OF GOD

The figure of Jesus Christ is probably the most recognized religious figure in today's world. Whether Jesus was a real man or the figment of imaginative religious writers, the mythology of this man has no doubt staked a place in our collective conscious. Millions of people adore, worship and pray to this figure everyday. What is it that makes Jesus's life and ministry so important? What does it mean that he was the "Son of God"?

An interpretation of the story of Jesus has been perpetuated by preachers and followers for centuries now. This interpretation focuses on the literal, with the events of Jesus's life deemed historical fact. Is it true that Jesus was the only Son of God and therefore the only divine being to ever grace this blessed Earth? The message has been repeated that if we do not take him as our personal savior we shall be condemned to an eternal afterlife of pain and suffering. Having faith and disbanding all rational and reason is the way in which one is to enter the gates of Heaven. What if this interpretation is wrong and if it is, would the power of the character of Jesus be then stripped?

Jesus was an example; the finest, most eloquent role model for the art of being. Christhood was something that anyone could achieve and Jesus "dying for our sins" was never intended to be an act done for the redemption of mankind, but rather an allegorical address to the evil tendencies that lay within each and every single human being. There have been numerous times in human history where people have simply fallen victim to the deadly sins that haunt the human vessel (our current age being one of them) and Jesus realizing his true potential and understanding the divine force that was within him was the ultimate allegory for those looking to combat those evils. Jesus woke up to the realization that he was, in fact, God. Gautama Siddartha had a similar experience in which he woke up to his true potential and divine nature and was given the title "Buddha" (Buddha literally means "the one who woke"). Leonardo Da Vinci, echoing Jesus and Buddha, once said, "I awoke, only to see the rest of the World was still asleep." This path of enlightenment is the same path that we all must follow and finding the God within is available to each and every person. Hermes informed us of this fact in the Corpus Hermeticum:

"If, then, thou dost not make thyself like unto God, thou canst not know Him. For like is knowable unto like."

71

The numerical equivalent of Jesus Christ is of grand importance in understanding the divinity of the name Jesus Christ.

JESUS CHRIST
45666 36 5567 = 59

Jesus sums to 27, Christ sums to 32 and together they add up to **59**. **59** is an important number for several reasons. There are **59** beads in a traditional Christian rosary and this is most assuredly the reason why. There are many important phrases that add up to **59**:

English Alphabet, Reborn Christian, In God We Trust,
The Holy Name of God, Alchemical Wedding, Alchemical Marriage

We can also find 59 in Pi. 3.14**159**. This connection to Pi may at first seem arbitrary until one adds up these 6 digits; 3+1+4+1+5+9 = 23. 23 is of course the numerical equivalent of Heaven. If we spell out the word "man" using our alphabet, climbing up to 7 and back down to 1 and then count the number of letters we used to do so, it will also equal 59.

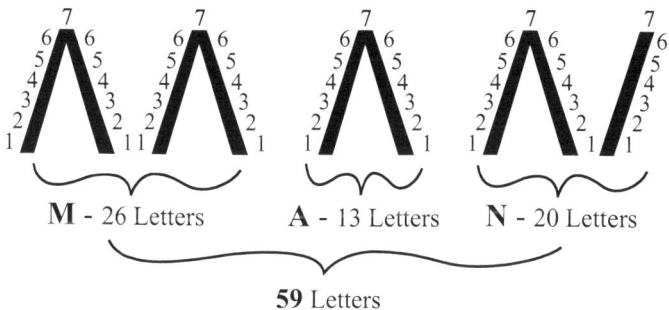

M - 26 Letters   A - 13 Letters   N - 20 Letters

59 Letters

Before Jesus became Jesus "Christ", he was Jesus of Nazareth or, in other words, he was a common "man". Man has a numerical equivalent of 3, which represents the Holy Trinity. To the ancients, the term "man" was not gender specific and was used to represent all of "mankind". "Nazareth" has a numerical equivalent of 27, which is the same as Christ symbolizing the 27 bones in the human hand. 27 is also a number seen in the Holy 108 (if we add the numbers divisible by a Trinity or 3 + 3 + 9 + 6 + 6 - see page 17) we yield the number 27. 27 is also a Trinity cubed, or 3 x 3 x 3. If we multiply the numerical equivalents of Jesus = 27 and Christ = 32 we yield the number **864** (27 x 32 = 864). The sun has a diameter of **864**,000 miles - surely not a coincidence.

72

The numerical equivalent of Jesus Christ has much more to offer. Let's look at the numbers of the Holy Name of JESUS.

JESUS
4 5 6 6 6

It is probably immediately apparent that Jesus encodes a very "beastly" number in his name and that is of course, **666**. This number is not a satanic or evil number at all as St. John informed us in Revelation 13:18, *"Here is wisdom.* Let him that hath understanding count the number of the beast for it is a number of man and his number *is* Six hundred three-score *and* six **(666)**." This number of wisdom is actually embedded in the divine 9 of our number line, known by the Greeks and Egyptians as the Ennead. The Ennead were the 9 gods or principals that governed the world through the laws of number. This "divine nine" is also celebrated in the Christian religion, mythologized in the Christian Angelic Hierarchy of 9 angels, separated into three levels: *3rd level*: Seraphim (9), Cherubim (8), Thrones (7), *2nd level*: Dominions (6), Virtues (5), Powers (4), *1st level*: Principalities (3), Archangels (2) and Angels (1). These 9 angels and their 3 levels leads us to the wise and holy number of 666 and consequently the 45 in the JE of Jesus Christ.

$$1 + 2 + 3 = 6 \qquad\qquad = 6$$
$$4 + 5 + 6 = 15 \text{ and } 1 + 5 = 6$$
$$7 + 8 + 9 = 24 \text{ and } 2 + 4 = 6$$
$$\boxed{45}$$

JE SUS
45 6 6 6

Now let's look at the numbers generated by the name CHRIST.

CHRIST
3 6 5 5 6 7

CHR yields us nothing less than the number of days in our solar year, or **365**. The next three numbers, when added, sum to 18 (5+6+7 =18). There are 18 years missing in the account of Jesus's life in the bible. Many believe that these years were spent traveling, mainly to Egypt, to learn the profound knowledge taught at the mystery schools. Whatever he did and wherever he was, after these 18 years Jesus realized and recognized his divine nature and spent his remaining time on the planet preaching it.

Christ equals 32 and Jesus lived 33 years after performing 33 miracles. These numbers are key to understanding one's inner god. There are 32 and 33 degrees in Freemasonry and this is exactly what these numbers refer to. One can rise in the ranks of Freemasonry and reach the 32nd degree by one's own accord, but one must be given the title, or anointed the 33rd degree. Christ literally translates to "The anointed one", which means that Christ, through his labor, love, altruism and *passion* climbed the Freemasonic ranks and fully recognized his divine nature - hence the attachment of the number 33 to his life.

Jesus Christ also encodes the Precession of the Equinoxes. If we multiply the numbers of Jesus (4x5x6x6x6 = 4,320) and add them to the multiplication of Christ (3x6x5x5x6x7 = 18,900) we yield the number 23,220. This is 2,700 years shy of one Precessional cycle of 25,920 years. The letters that were above Christ when he was crucified were INRI (Which translates to; "Jesus of Nazareth, King of the Jews"). In Hebrew, these 4 letters added up to 270. 270 x 10, or our base ten, equals 2,700.

י נ ר י

INRI

(**I**) Yod = 10, (**N**) Nun = 50, (**R**) Resh = 200 (**I**) Yod = 10
= **270**

This 270 can also be found in the divine 9 or the Christian Angelic Hierarchy. If we separate our divine 9 into 3 levels, this time not in their numerical order but instead by a separation of 3, (the separations being 1, 4, 7 / 2, 5, 8 / 3, 6, 9) and then we multiply and add their sums together, we yield the number 270.

$$1 \times 4 \times 7 = 28$$
$$2 \times 5 \times 8 = 80$$
$$3 \times 6 \times 9 = 162$$
$$\overline{\mathbf{270}}$$

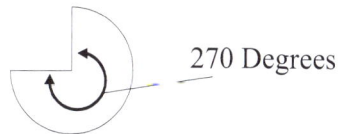

270 Degrees

270 degrees is nothing more than 3/4 of a circle and this is a undoubtedly a reference to the sacred geometrical 3, meaning Heaven, over the 4 representing Earth.

Worshiping the solar deity of Jesus was not intended to be the worship of a singular divine man but instead the metaphorical focus one could utilize to unearth the spiritual essence and light that lay within every single man, woman and child who graces this great Earth.

74

THE "UNLUCKY" NUMBER 13

In psychology there is a condition known as Triskaidekaphobia, which is a fear of the number 13. 13 has long been considered a superstitious and "unlucky" number. Many buildings around the world have been built without a 13th floor. This superstition stems from an occurrence on the night of Friday the 13th, October 1307 when the Phillip IV of France ordered the arrests of the Knights Templar. The Knights Templar went underground after this night after and many believe that they later reformed and developed their organization into the Freemasonic brotherhood that exists today. The Knights Templar were said to hold the secrets of the Holy Grail and the secret knowledge that was taught in the Pythagorean and Egyptian schools; a body of knowledge based on symbol, number and allegory. Arresting and ultimately murdering these Knights on that fateful 13th day in October was undoubtedly a symbolic act on the part of Philip IV. Friday the 13th happens on average about 3 times per year; again a reference to the Holy Trinity. 13 just may have been one of the most important and holy numbers to the Knights Templar and therefore why this date became important.

Many important words in our cipher add up to 13:
John, Pope, Lord, God, Sun, Psalm, Nile

In our cipher we separated the alphabet into two blocks of 13 letters, A - M and N - Z. The Freemasonic symbol of the compass and square with the "G" in the center helped us establish this cryptogram. The "G" is the 7th letter of the alphabet and is resonant with the Sabbath, or the day in which God rested and the letter that we "rested" on in our alphabet to walk back down.

13 Letters   **13** Letters

A B C D E F G H I J K L M   N O P Q R S T U V W X Y Z
1 2 3 4 5 6 7 6 5 4 3 2 1   1 2 3 4 5 6 7 6 5 4 3 2 1

This "unlucky" number 13 was necessary to focus on in order to establish the cipher for our alphabet. Could it be that Philip IV wanted to keep this knowledge for himself and his royal bloodline and out of the hands of those who went throughout the land teaching it to worthy initiates? We can only speculate on this matter. Whatever knowledge the Knights Templar held, it was of such importance that their arrests and deaths were warranted and occurred on none other than Friday the *13th*.

The number 13 is also imbedded in the sacred geometrical construction called Metatron's Cube. Metatron's Cube is a two-dimensional geometric figure created from 13 equal circles. 6 circles are placed in a hexagonal pattern around a central circle with 6 more extending out along the same radial lines. It is 12 spheres around 1, reflecting the 12 hours of a clock as well as Jesus and his 12 disciples. Metatron's Cube is considered one of the most holy of the ancient sacred geometrical symbols and one that encodes the 5 Platonic solids. The Platonic solids are the 5 polygons that can be constructed within a sphere and are named after the Greek philosopher Plato. Metatron's Cube is directly related to the Holy 108 of Phi as shown below.

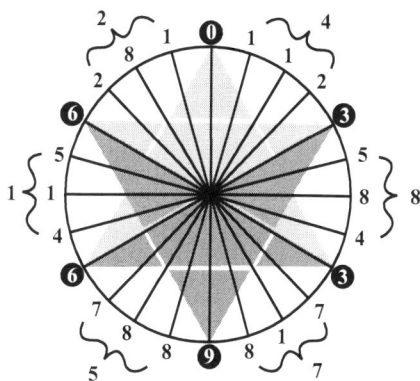

Metatron's Cube   The Holy 108

Tetrahedron   Hexahedron   Octahedron   Dodechahedron   Isocohedron
               (Cube)

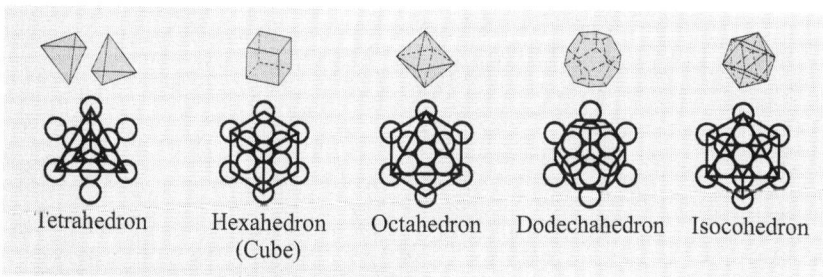

The 12 disciples around Christ in Leonardo Da Vinci's *The Last Supper* symbolizes not only Metatron's Cube and the Holy 108 but also the 12 ages of the Zodiac with *you*, or the central Christ figure, sitting in its center.

Plato believed that the 4 elements of air, fire, earth and water were constructed using these 5 polygons. The entrance to the Platonic schools read "Let none ignorant of geometry enter here." In order for one to understand God, or the Grand Architect, and the world he created, one would undoubtedly need an intimate knowledge of geometry.

Metatron is mentioned in the Pseudepigrapha and most prominently in the Hebrew Merkabah Book of Enoch. The book describes the link between Enoch, son of Jared (great grandfather of Noah) and his transformation into the angel Metatron. His grand title was "the lesser YHWH". This 13 sphered geometrical symbol incorporates two very profound ideas: the *Seal* of Solomon, with the maxim of "As above, so below." and the Hermetic *Seal* lauded by the alchemists. The Hermetic Seal can be found by connecting the numbers we found in our division of 360 degrees by 7 or 1, 4, 2, 8, 5, 7 and 1, the very same sequence that gave us our "Symbol of Enlightenment". (This can be found by reducing the numbers between the 3, 6, 9 and 0 down to their decimal parity equivalents)

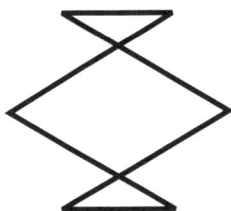

Seal of Solomon   The Hermetic *Seal*

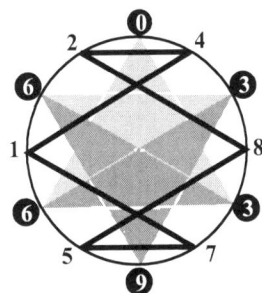

As we saw earlier, a pentagram with a circle ratio of 13, each arm of the star will equal 12.36 or the number of lunar months, days and hours in a solar year. Add the arms together and you get the number of full moons in 5 years. In looking back at the lunar calendar encoded in Stonehenge and the added multiplication of Jachin and Boaz, we found the number 364, which constitutes a perfect calendar of 13 months of 28 days each. We also found this calendar in the deck of cards with 13 cards per suit as well as in the great Mayan pyramid of Chichen Itza. 13 is not a number to be feared but instead a number to be revered. According to Stonehenge, Jachin and Boaz, the Mayans and the deck of cards, 13 is a *magical number* that allows one to easily map the cycles of the heavens. It is also the number of our *Sun* and our *Lord*.

THE MYTH OF ER

The alchemists and so many of our ancient ancestors believed that the world was crafted and constructed using four basic elements. These elements represented the phases that everything in the natural world undergoes. In the English language we know these elements to be Earth, Water, Air and Fire. Modern science has a similar concepts for the substantiation of all matter: Solid, Liquid, Gas and Plasma. It seems that the alchemists of old and the modern mind may have had more in common than we tend to believe as these words seem to have almost identical definitions. Earth - Solid, Water - Liquid, Air - Gas and Fire - Plasma.

The Myth of Er is a story that concludes Plato's highly acclaimed work, *The Republic*. The story is the tale of a Greek man named "Er", and recounts his travels through the afterlife. It introduces the idea that moral people are rewarded and immoral people punished after death. The story is highly allegorical, highly numerical and deals with concepts like the astral plane and reincarnation. Why did Plato choose to name his inter-dimensionally traveling lead character, Er?

Sound out the four elements that the alchemists believed made up the natural world and the answer becomes immediately clear.

Erth   wat**Er**   a**Er**   fi**Er**

Cymatics is the modern science of creating geometric structure and form through vibration. If sound is indeed the force that created the universe, then the sound of **ER** must have an enormous significance. The sum of the numerical equivalents of Earth Water, Air and Fire add up to **78**.

EARTH	WATER	AIR	FIRE
5 1 5 7 6	4 1 7 5 5	1 5 5	6 5 5 5 = **78**

In the song "The Twelve Days of Christmas" there are **78** gifts given by one's true love. A traditional Tarot deck contains 21 trump cards, the Fool and the 56 suit cards for a total of **78** cards. 78 divided by our Holy Trinity = **26**. This gives us an alphabet for each of the members of our Holy Trinity; 26 for the Father, 26 for the Son and 26 for the Holy Spirit. We will delve much deeper into these concepts in Volume 2 of this text.

78

THE RAINBOW BRIDGE

The rainbow is a natural phenomena adored by peoples the world over. The Norse claimed that it was the bridge between Heaven and Earth and the Irish believed that a pot of gold could be found at its end. The rainbow, in all of its magic and austerity, elucidates several core truths about the nature of existence with its awesome display of circular vibration. The numerical equivalent of "Rainbow" sums to 20.

RAINBOW
5 1 51 2 2 4 = **20**

The seven colors of the rainbow, or sometimes abbreviated by the acronym Roy G Biv, when added together sum to **140**.

RED	ORANGE	YELLOW	GREEN	BLUE	INDIGO	VIOLET
5 5 4	2 5 1 1 7 5	2 5 2 2 2 4	7 5 5 5 1	2 2 6 5	5 1 4 5 7 2	5 5 2 2 5 7

If we divide **140** by our RAINBOW, or **20**, we yield the holy number 7. 140/20 = 7. 7 is of course nothing more than the number of colors in the rainbow itself and the number of letters in the word. **140** x **20** = 2,800. This divided by 7 equals <u>400</u> (2,800 / 7 = <u>400</u>). The Sun is <u>400</u> times larger than the Moon. (Sun) 864,000 miles / <u>400</u> = 2,160 miles (Moon)

The geometry of the rainbow was most assuredly understood by many cultures before embedded in the number **42**. 3 was often considered the first number of manifestation because it is the first number than encapsulates any space (1 and 2 are merely points / lines) and three, adding through our divine nine, equals 42. (3 + 4 + 5 + 6 + 7 + 8 + 9 = **42**) There are **42** principles of Ma'at (where we derive the word "math"), the Ancient Egyptian personification of law, order and truth. **42** is the number with which God creates the Universe in Kabbalistic tradition and the Gutenberg Bible had **42** lines per page. **42** is also the answer to life according to Douglas Adams in his book "The Hitchhiker's Guide to the Galaxy". The position of a rainbow in the sky is always in the opposite direction of the Sun with respect to the observer creating two angels both of 42 degrees.

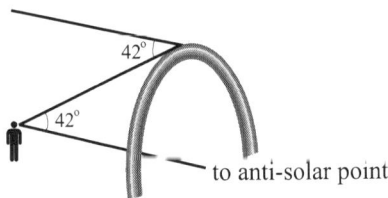

79

ABRACADABRA!

The ancient art of magic has been recognized in almost every single culture throughout history. Magic is considered by modern science as nothing more than slight of hand tricks instituted by clever people on an unsuspecting or naive audience. Is the explanation as simple as that? The art of magic was often done by casting a "spell". This phrase is interesting. Are casting a "spell" and the workings of number and letter in the art of gematria one and the same art? Does "spell"ing a particular word with particular sounds in a particular order somehow manifest an intention by the one casting this "spell"? The most famous word for casting a spell is ABRACADBRA.

The sum of Abracadabra equals 26, which reflects the number of characters in the English Alphabet, the numerical equivalent of the word "Numbers" as well as the Hebraic Tetragrammaton. If we split up Abracadabra into 3 sections, reflective of the Holy Trinity, it reveals the esoteric mathematical doctrines adored throughout the ages; Pi and Squaring the Circle.

ABRA	CADA	BRA
1 2 5 1	3 1 4 1	2 5 1 = **26**
(9)	π	8

SQUARING THE CIRCLE

Circle of **9**: $\pi \times 4.5^2 = 63.64$

Square of **8**: $8^2 = 64$

"ABRA" sums to 9 and "BRA" sums to 8, which represents the circle of 9 and the square of 8 in the mystical act of Squaring the Circle. There are also 4 letters in ABRA representing Earth and 3 in BRA representing Heaven. Between Heaven and Earth is nothing more than the Holy ratio of Pi, or 3.141. Notice "RA" or the Egyptian sun god, is located twice in the word. The sun is, of course, a star and it seems that Abracadabra is, in fact, encoding a commandment. Its magic is informing you what to do and that is:

Speak the Alphabet (**AB**) of the Sun (**RA**), which can be decoded with PI (**CADA**) and you will be (**B**) a Sun (**RA**) - you will become enlightened.

As it turns out, there is nothing more magical in this world than the very words we speak. Casting a spell is manifesting, through intention and the magic of language, the world that you wish to perceive. Just ask the gospel. (GO SPELL!)

THE SUPREME BEING

In Freemasonry, many of the most famous works, such as Albert Pike's *Morals and Dogma*, often refer to an entity entitled the "Supreme Being". Knowing the nature of the mysteries surrounding Freemasonry and their many-layered meanings, we should not immediately see this title as only a reference to god. The idea of the "Supreme Being" was not intended to be something one should worship but instead a state of grace that one should work towards. The idea was to recognize the "supreme being" of oneself and to understand one's own divine nature. The numerical equivalent of "Supreme Being" equals 51 and this number, as we will see, has a deep meaning shared by alchemists, kabbalists, Egyptians and Freemasons alike.

SUPREME BEING
6 6 3 5 5 1 5 2 5 5 1 7 = **51**

The alchemists and the kabbalists both shared a worship for the supreme symbol of the Tetragrammaton. This Holy Name of God was used by the Kabbalists in their study of the Torah and the Zohar and may very well be the "Lost Masonic Word" of the Freemasons. In our cipher, we used the Tetragrammaton to understand the gematria of the English Alphabet by connecting the non-prime numbers and dividing them by the central 7 in our alphabet to find Pi on both sides of our alphabet. This Holy Name of God added up to 26 in the Hebrew cipher, which is a direct correlation to the number of letters in the English Alphabet. In our cipher the "Lost Masonic Word" of this "Supreme Being" known as the "Tetragrammaton" finds us 51 once again.

TETRAGRAMMATON   LOST MASONIC WORD
7 5 7 5 1 7 5 1 1 1 1 7 2 1 = **51**   2 2 6 7 1 1 6 2 1 5 3 4 2 5 4 = **51**

The alchemists of old touted and revered two concepts that both sum to 51. The first is known as the magical potion of immortality called the "Elixir of Life". The elixir of life, to many of the Theosophists, was one's own spinal fluid, that travels a path from one's root chakra to one's crown, passing through the seven stages of spiritual enlightenment. Philosophically, this fluid could be the innate understanding of the fluidity of everything in nature. This idea is echoed by the Greek philosopher Heraclitus in his famous statement "all flows". Everything in nature is in a constant state of simultaneous growth and decay. Understanding this concept may have made it easier for one to "go with the flow" in life and quite possibly even in the afterlife.

The second concept that equals 51 was called the "Universal Panacea" and it was deemed the universal remedy that could heal the ills of the world. The Tetragrammaton and the Universal Panacea were most likely one and the same in that once the Holy Name of God was understood, man could no longer be without God and only then could he see him and his eternal works in every written word. The act of moving around a sacred object is known as "circumambulation" and it equals **51** as well. Our holy geometric symbol of "Metatron's Cube" equals **51**. The word "philosophers" also equals **51**, and if the Earth was made up of *Philosophers* understanding the *Universal Panacea* through the magic of the *Tetragrammaton*, we might just live in a sane and beautiful world.

The question is of course, why 51?

As we have seen previously, 360 degrees of a circle can be divided by our base ten system evenly, except by our holy number 7. This division not only yields us the decimal numbers of 1, 4, 2, 8, 5, 7 and 1 making up the "Symbolof Enlightenment" but it also presents us with the answer to our question.

$$360 / 7 = \underline{\mathbf{51}}.428571$$

The Great Pyramid of Giza encodes many mathematical concepts such as Phi and Pi and has a slope of roughly 51 degrees and 51minutes. In order to "Square the Circle" and find the radii of both the Moon and the Earth, this angle of **51** degrees and **51** minutes was absolutely necessary to build into the pyramid's architecture. Without it, the Egyptians would have been off in the measurements of these two heavenly bodies and the Egyptians were hardly ever mistaken when it came to their mathematics and geometry.

Two of the most revered deities in the Egyptian theology were Isis and Osiris. These two characters, as we have seen, were akin to Adam and Eve in the Holy Bible. Not only could we find Pi within the mythology of Isis and Osiris, but as it turns out, these two deities also give us that magic number 51.

ISIS   OSIRIS
5656 + 2 65556 = 51

With the application of mirroring, 51 now becomes 15.

82

THE SUPREME MIND

In our cipher, many common words dealing with divinity are attached to the number 15.

Symbol, Human, Good, Gold, Flame, Word, Math

The Ankh, (⚲) known as the key of life, was a talisman most often adorned by the Egyptians. The Ankh was known as the "crux ansata" and has its most direct correlation to the Christian cross. The Ankh translated to "Enkh" in English and sums to 15.

The word "nous", coined by the Greeks, meant divine mind or common sense and it also equals 15. The Pythagorean Tetractys, a mathematical idea celebrated by those initiated into the Pythagorean Mystery Schools, is the numbers 1, 2, 3 and 4 stacked up together to make a pyramid. Added together, these first four numbers in our number line equal 10, referencing our base 10 system. If we added the next sequential number, or 5, we end up with our mighty 15 whilst still maintaining pyramidal form. This pyramid of 15 encases a smaller pyramid of three, representing the Holy Trinity coming together as one, giving us once again, 12 around 1.

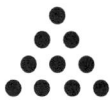

The Tetractys   15 - "Twelve around One"

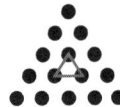

Where the number 15 is most important is where we find it in our number line. If we walk up our number line, we find that 15 actual caps off the first 5 digits of Pi.

0 1 2 3 4 5 6 7 8 9 10 11 12 13**1415** 16 17 18...

Take heed though, for just like all things in the experiential world, duality reigns supreme and therefore 15 is not only the source of "Good" and "Gold" but also the source of the devil. "Hell" sums to 15 and the 15th card of the tarot deck is "The Devil" whose charms every "human" is subjected to.

THE DEVIL.

THE RECURRING NUMBER 14

There were **14** stations, or "ways of the cross", in the Passion of Jesus. Osiris was cut into **14** sections by his evil twin Set. There are **14** sections of your five fingers. The "full moon cycle" is a cycle of **14** lunations. A whole number equivalent of Pi can be found by dividing 44 by **14** equaling 3.142. Why **14**?

The human body can be divided into 14 sections of Phi and Phee. Ideally this is done with 7 sections, but since both 1 and .618 make up the ratio, this division of 7 can be doubled to express both parts of the ratio. The division of Osiris in the myth expresses the ratio of Phi in the human body and his godliness a reflection of the perfection and sacred nature of the human form.

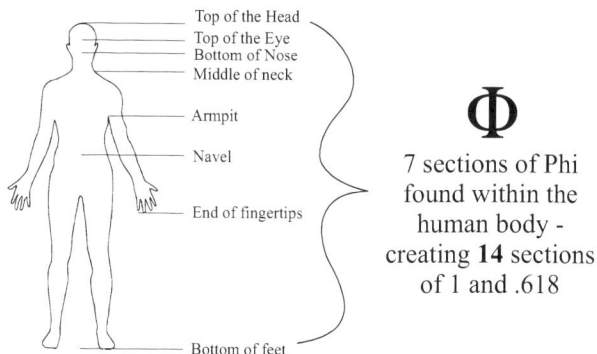

Top of the Head
Top of the Eye
Bottom of Nose
Middle of neck

Armpit

Navel

End of fingertips

Bottom of feet

Φ

7 sections of Phi found within the human body - creating **14** sections of 1 and .618

360 degrees of a circle multiplied by 14 equals 5,040, or the combined radius of the Earth and Moon in miles.

Jesus's "Crucifixion" preceded his "Last Supper."

CRUCIFIXION	LAST SUPPER
3 5 6 3565 352 1 = **44**	2 1 67 6 63 35 5 = **44**

The Last Supper, the famous painting by Leonardo Da Vinci, shows Jesus and his twelve disciples gathering together for Jesus's last meal. Between Jesus's "Last Supper" and "Crucifixion" were what was known as the **14** stations of the cross or Jesus's *passion*. 44/14 = 3.142 or Pi.

Where 14 makes its most grand appearance is how it is found right outside the Garden of Eden, where it helps construct that holy ratio of Pi.

THE GARDEN OF EVEN

In Genesis Adam and Eve were together in the Garden of Eden. They were equals in the garden, naked and unashamed until one day a serpent tempted them to eat the forbidden fruit from the Tree of the Knowledge of Good and Evil. And ever since that fateful day we have been cast out of the garden. Are we forever banned from the Garden or can we somehow find our way back to the symbiotic state that Man once shared with nature and with God? To somehow think that this story is a literal account of historical events seems quite absurd. But if we understand this story mathematically, suddenly the characters and plot shed a whole new light.

Adam is a reference to the "Odd" numbers, 1, 3, 5, 7 and 9 and Eve is of course a reference to the Even numbers, 2, 4, 6, 8 and 10. In order to encapsulate our base ten system, we can make Adam 01, or *zero and the first odd number* and we can assign Eve 10, or the last even number making Adam and Eve reflections of each other.

Adam / Odd = $\boxed{01 \mid 10}$ = Eve / Even

If Adam and Eve were once equal inside the Garden of *Even* then Adam as **01** was equal to Eve as **10**. 01 = 10. If we add these two characters together we get the number Eleven. 01 + 10 =11. Eleven is an interesting word because not only does it sum to our heavenly number 23, but EL is a name for God and EVEN means *equality*. Put these words together and we can find our Garden of Eden or GOD is EVEN. The number 11 is of course nothing more than an equal sign (=) standing upright. The reason that Adam was the first being created and Eve carved out of his rib refers to the fact that the first number in our number line is an odd number, with Eve, or the next number, 2, being even. It's as simple as that. The multiplication of the numbers 1 - 10 by our divine 9 finds us the most interesting congruence. Our number line can be divided between 5 and 6, with each sum being the mirror of its corresponding number as shown below.

9 x 10 = 90	09 = 1 x 9
9 x 9 = 81	18 = 2 x 9
9 x 8 = 72	27 = 3 x 9
9 x 7 = 63	36 = 4 x 9
9 x 6 = 54	45 = 5 x 9

This mirroring represents the reigning concept of the Garden of Eden, and the philosophical truth shared by all the sages of old; The Unity of Opposites. Man and woman are equal. Odd and even are equal. Continuity is impossible without it. If we walk up the number line, out of our base 10 system and to the numbers 11, 12 and 13, we find this mirroring continues if we square these three numbers and their mirrors (12 becomes 21, 13 becomes 31).

$11^2 = 121$	$121 = 11^2$
$12^2 = 144$	$441 = 21^2$
$13^2 = 169$	$961 = 31^2$

If we walk up to our recurring number 14, mirror it to become 41 and square both the numbers, we find the mirroring stops. ($196 = 14^2$ | $41^2 = 1681$) If you notice this is also the place where we find the decimal place in Pi.

11 12 13 **.14**15

This entire concept can be elucidated in the classic symbol encoding the philosophy of the Unity of Opposites, the Chinese Yin Yang.

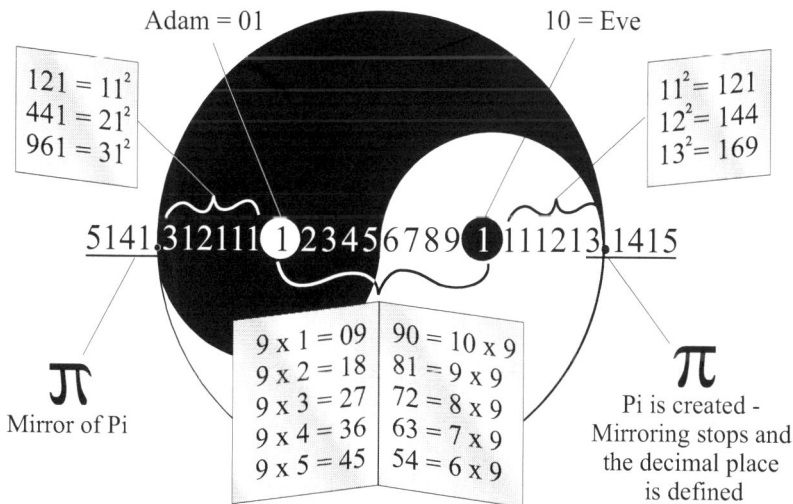

Adam = 01   10 = Eve

$121 = 11^2$
$441 = 21^2$
$961 = 31^2$

$11^2 = 121$
$12^2 = 144$
$13^2 = 169$

5141.312111①123456789①111213.1415

 Π
Mirror of Pi

$9 \times 1 = 09$	$90 = 10 \times 9$
$9 \times 2 = 18$	$81 = 9 \times 9$
$9 \times 3 = 27$	$72 = 8 \times 9$
$9 \times 4 = 36$	$63 = 7 \times 9$
$9 \times 5 = 45$	$54 = 6 \times 9$

π
Pi is created -
Mirroring stops and
the decimal place
is defined

Adam and Eve were cast out of the Garden by eating the forbidden fruit, representing Original Sin. This temptation was of course induced by the serpent, "more subtil than any beast in the field". It does not take much imagination to recognize that "Original Sin" is simply the "Origins of Sine". Sine and cosine are the height and base of a right triangle in a circle of radius 1 as shown below. Sine and cosine is the first function in trigonometry and is visually two lines, snaking out of Pi. This idea is reflected in the Pi verse, or **3:14,** in Genesis: "And the LORD God said unto the serpent, because you have done this, you are cursed above all cattle, and above every beast of the field; *upon thy belly shalt you go*, and dust shalt you eat all the days of your life."

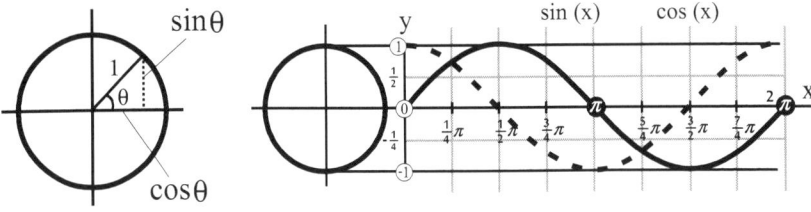

The sine wave function can be understood much easier when using the Greek letter Tau or "T" *instead of pi!* The "T" symbol has long been assoc-iated with man and one used by the Freemasons. Tau is known as the ratio of any circle's circumference to its radius (equal to 2π or 6.28). Since we use the *radius* with our compass to draw a circle, and *not the diameter*, it seems most appropriate to use this function for it makes the math much more eloquent.

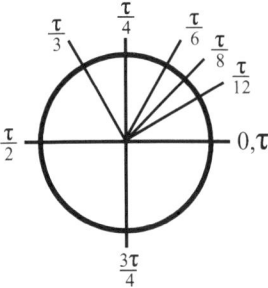

$T\tau$ The Greek letter "Tau"

τ Tau vs. π Pi
Example:
$\pi / 2$ becomes $\tau / 4$
$\pi / 4$ becomes $\tau / 8$ etc.

This separation by the serpent, or the Sine wave, is also found in the Yin Yang symbol. Yin being female (Eve) and Yang being male (Adam). Both Yin and Yang swirl around each other separated by the serpent. The Yin Yang symbol, in all of its simplicity, actual encodes the mythological and mathematical concepts of creation.

Making the correlation to Adam being odd and Eve being even, we can now reference the mythology of them being "cast out" of the Garden of Eden and focus on the 8 numbers we have left, or 2 - 9. These 8 numbers are reflected in the Buddhist Noble Eightfold Path. This number 8 is also seen in how we naturally cut a *pi*zza. This division also gives us the four fundamental symbols we use in mathematics:

 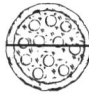  

Add   Subtract   Multiply   Divide

If we cast out Adam and Eve, or 01 and 10 and place these 8 numbers within our divided Pi, the mythology of the Garden of Eden provides us with the most useful information.

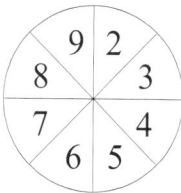

Adam = 01 | 10 = Eve
Cast out of the Garden of Eden

If we multiply each of these numbers by our divine 9 and add their sum, it will give us the number **396**. (18+27+36+45+54+63+72+81 = 396) 396 x 10 equals **3,960** or the radius of the Earth in miles.

If we multiply each of these numbers by 12, or find their equivalents in inches and then add these up, we yield the number **528**. (24+36+48+60+72+84+96+108 = 528) 528 x 10 equals **5,280** or the number of feet in an English mile.

If we multiply the numbers across each other and then add their sums, it equals **100**, resonating with the 3 great crosses in the sky; the Seasonal Cross, the Daily Cross and the Galactic Cross. (18+24+28+30 = **100**)

If we add the entire Pi together (2+3+4+5+6+7+8+9) it sums to 44. If we use the letter "D" as our guide, representing the "Delta" or 4th letter of the alphabet, and add up the right side of our Pi (2+3+4+5) equaling 14, we can find a whole number equivalent of Pi or 44/14 = **3.142**.

The letter D becomes very important in understanding the myth of the Garden of Eden. "D", like the Delta, is the fourth letter of the alphabet and encodes our base ten system (1+2+3+4 =10), expressed through the Pythagorean Tetractys.

The number 4 and hence the "D" is also a reference to the creation of the Earth through the sacred geometrical concepts of Heaven being 3 and Earth being 4. A Delta is a land mass that is formed at the mouth of a river, where that river flows into an ocean. The Delta, symbolically, is our Earth formed by the mouth of the river of the lord. The D also references the diameter one needs to find the ratio of Pi. The Sun rising on the horizon (or "Horus Rising") creates a "D" giving us the *diameter of the Sun.* And as we have previously seen "Horizon" equals 22 and has 7 letters finding us once again that illuminating ratio of Pi.

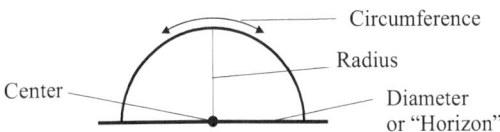

The letter "**D**"

HORIZON
6 2 5 5 1 2 1 = **22**

We use the radius to find the circumference of a circle, but we *double the radius* to find Pi, or the ratio of a circle's circumference *to its diameter.* The symbolism of the letter D is a direct reflection of this mathematical fact. The plural of radius is *radii,* the "I" and "I" no doubt references to man and woman. The letter D, by its simple construction and where it is placed in our alphabet, informs us of the basic mathematical principles we need to understand the creation of our Earth.

$$\Delta\delta$$

The 4th letter of the Greek alphabet, Delta was represented by two symbols; a triangle and an egg with a serpent emerging. The Delta seems to have been caused by a serpent, cracking the primordial egg of creation as the virgin birth that opened wide the mouth of river of the lord.

THE PRIMORDIAL EGG

The world egg, or cosmic egg, is a mythological motif found in the creation stories of many cultures and civilizations. Typically, the world egg is a beginning of some sort, and the Universe or some primordial being comes into existence by "hatching" from the egg, sometimes lain on the primordial waters of the Earth.

The Indian Rig Veda calls the source of the Universe Hiranyagarbha, which literally means "Golden Fetus" or "Golden Womb". This Golden Womb has been geometrically symbolized by the Vesica Piscis, which translates to "Vessel of the fish" and is where we derive the symbol for the Jesus fish.

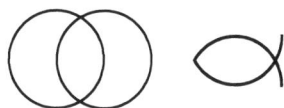

The Upanishads elaborate that the Hiranyagarbha floated around in emptiness for a while and then broke into two halves which formed Dyaus (Heaven) and Prithvi (Earth)   In the myth of Pangu, developed by Taoist monks, the Universe began as an Egg. The earliest ideas of an egg-shaped cosmos come from some of the Sanksrit scriptures. Sanskrit is the earliest form of language known to mankind. The Sanksrit term for the Egg is Brahmanda (Brahm - "Cosmos" or "Expanding" / Anda - "Egg")

Modern science explains that everything in the Universe is the result of a massive explosion called the big bang and before this big bang everything in the Universe was concealed in what is sometimes called the "Primordial Atom" which echoes the fundamental idea of the primordial egg. This egg was encoded into the nursery rhyme of *Humpty Dumpty* and shares the same story line of the Egyptian Eye of Horus myth - an irreparable egg or eye that was once whole but one day cracked. The primordial egg motif is akin to the Garden of Eden as well with the "*fall*" of mankind being akin to the "*fall*" and cracking of the egg. The purpose of these stories and myths is to challenge the reader: get back to the Garden by making man and woman equals. Realize you are the "missing" fraction of the Eye of Horus and piece it back together. Out of all the king's horses and all the king's men, *you are the one* who can put Humpty Dumpty back on his wall.

THE SERPENT IN THE SKY

Serpent symbolism and worship has been the focus of so many civilizations throughout history that it is next to impossible to find a civilization that does not have some reference to snakes. Eastern, Western and native cultures the world over are richly embedded with serpents and dragon symbolism. Interestingly, they are often seen as both evil and symbols of wisdom and power.

In the south west corner of Ohio is an ancient mound made into the formation of a serpent who is in the processing of biting into an egg. This mound is built up around a geomagnetic hot spot and it is unclear as to what culture formed this mound and how they did it. This Serpent Mound seems to be telling a story, quite possibly of cosmic origin. Could the primordial egg of creation have been cracked by a wise, tempting serpent?

THE SERPENT MOUND, SERPENT MOUND PARK, NEAR LOUDON, ADAMS COUNTY, OHIO.

In the biblical myth, Adam and Eve were together in the Garden of Eden until the serpent, or sine wave, tempted them by "original sin". This egg, or Garden of Eden, was separated and mankind has been cast out into a world of dualities, or of good and evil, ever since. We can understand the less dire nature of this myth if we understand that *fruit* etymologically means enjoyment and that original sin *granted us knowledge*, the fruit or enjoyment of consciousness and the ability to know the difference between good and evil. The only detriment to eating the fruit of the Tree of the Knowledge of Good and Evil was that we would "surely die". The snake was powerful enough to tempt all of mankind and we have been fighting with him ever since. In Hinduism, Kundalini is the yogic divinatory practice of raising this all-powerful snake up one's spine and through one's chakras to obtain enlightenment. The snake is only dangerous if you don't know how to handle it. The same poison from the snake's bite that can kill you, is also the anti-venom.

The Earth traces out an imaginary circle in the heavens as it points to different pole stars in its course through the 25,920 year period of the precession of the equinoxes. This circle traced out in the heavens is said to be done by a continuous wobble of the Earth on its axis, though this hasn't been confirmed. Several researchers believe that we are in a binary orbit with the star Sirius, the brightest star in the night sky, and hence why this ancient star has been the focus of veneration by cultures like the Egyptians, Greeks, Dogon and Pawnee. Sirius, as we know, shares the same 365.24 day solar year that we do. Our current pole star, the star approximately aligned with the Earth's axis of rotation, is Polaris, a part of the constellation Ursa Minor. Within the path of the pole star sits the constellation Draco, which is Latin for Dragon. Draco is a circumpolar constellation, which means it never sets and is always viewable to those in the Northern hemisphere. This large constellation is a mythologized dragon that forever rotates within the path of the North Celestial Pole. This Dragon in the castle of the Heavens above is tempting you, the warrior, to slay it. The snake points the way to the Heavenly axis upon which all of the universe spins. Finding the center, or the axis mundi, grants the person the privilege of getting off the Wheel of Karma and Wheel of Fortune and into the center, onto the Merkabah, or the chariot throne of God.

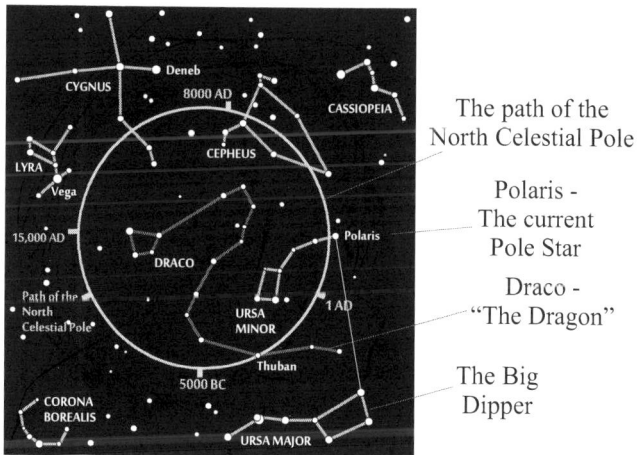

The path of the North Celestial Pole

Polaris - The current Pole Star

Draco - "The Dragon"

The Big Dipper

Another symbolic serpent seen in the sky is the alchemical serpent Ouroboros, which is seen eating its own tail to form our very own Milky Way galaxy.

Above is a picture of our Milky Way Galaxy. If one looks closely, one can see a snake head eating its tail in the cloudy, milky star matter that forms our galaxy. Without the light pollution of our modern cities, the peoples of the past could easily see much more of the Galaxy and therefore pick out peculiar qualities within its structure. The snake eating its tail speaks of the cyclical nature of all things in existence, from the seasons of the year to the process of one's birth from the abyss to the ultimate return to that abyss upon one's death. The process of self-regeneration symbolized by the snake eating its own tail reminds one of another structure resembling snakes: DNA.

DNA, or deoxribonucleic acid, contains the genetic structure than makes up all living things. DNA's two polymer strands resemble two snakes twisting around each other. Like the Ouroboros, DNA self-replicates, or can make copies of itself, thus regenerating itself. These two snakes wrapped around each other has been symbolized by the Caduceus, or staff of Hermes, and is a symbol for health and vitality. It is highly likely that the Greeks, Egyptians and alchemists of the past were acutely aware of DNA's structure and its importance for life on Earth. With an imaginative and keen eye, one can almost see the mouth and eyes of the serpent in the cross section of DNA shown above.

If we take the Hermetic maxim of "As above, so below" to heart, we should understand that any serpent that lies in the heavens, must also lie within us.

93

666 - THE BEAST WITHIN

As we saw within the name of Jesus, and as told to us by St. John in his Revelation, 666 is number assigned to those with wisdom. 666 was deemed "*a number of man*" as well as a "*number of the beast*". What was St. John saying here? If 666 was a number for man and beast, *was man therefore the beast*? This beast within was symbolized by a serpent. This is the same serpent that was "more subtil than any beast of the field," that God put in the Garden of Eden to tempt mankind. The serpent was known to be the source of one's spiritual powers in many cultures. It was simultaneously one's worst nightmare and one's finest hour. We understood that 666 was encoded within the *divine nine* of the Greek and Egyptian Ennead, or simply the numbers 1 - 9 separated into a trinity.

$$1 + 2 + 3 = \textbf{6} \qquad 4 + 5 + 6 = 15 \ \& \ 1 + 5 = \textbf{6} \qquad 7 + 8 + 9 = 24 \ \& \ 2 + 4 = \textbf{6}$$

These 9 numbers were mythologized in numerous ways. Hinduism speaks of the "nine cobras of brahma" and the Cabbala refers to the 9 legions of angels that dance about the throne of the hidden god. The Mayan serpent god Kukulcan travels down the steps of a 9 level pyramid by shadow and light on the solstices and equinoxes. The highest angel in the Christian angelic hierarchy was known as the Seraphim and etymologically means "flying serpent" or "winged serpent". This high-flying, fiery angelic serpent is akin to the dragon celebrated in many Eastern traditions. In our Holy 108 of Phi, the first 24 number sequence adds up to 108, with every subsequent cycle adding up to 117. The Chinese dragon was said to have 117 scales, which is an obvious reference to this repeating cycle in the Fibonacci Sequence. Taming the serpent within was part of the alchemical training. The serpent could cause much pain by tempting one with greed, egotism, power and arrogance and yet it could send one to the highest of heights, into the heavens of truth. Slaying or taming this dragon or serpent was the hero's journey. The entire story of the warrior journeying across far lands to a castle to then fight a dragon and rescue a princess is nothing more than an allegory for the internal struggle one undertakes when trying to complete the alchemical work. The princess is the helpless counterpart that the dragon has captured and taken hostage inside the castle walls of one's ego. In order to merge the halves of oneself, a dragon would need to be overcome. The alchemical marriage could not be performed without it.

THE CADUCEUS

The Caduceus was another symbol widely used by the alchemists and Egyptians and one that symbolized health and vitality. The Caduceus is still used today as the main symbol for the medical field. This symbol was most often symbolized as two snakes wrapped around a central staff, rising up to a sphere with two wings.

The winged globe, or sphere, was a symbol used consistently throughout Egypt and was most likely a symbol denoting enlightenment. Many have postulated that the Caduceus is a direct reference to the double-helix structure of DNA, the genetic structure within all life. Without question the Egyptians were an advanced civilization, who mastered the arts of medicine, architecture, mathematics and symbolism. The Caduceus, and many variations of serpents wrapped around staffs, are seen throughout the ancient world, especially in Greece and most often symbolized intelligence and divinity. If we look at the numerical equivalent of Caduceus, the first thing one might notice is the first three letters are those recurring digits of Pi. **3.14**

CADUCEUS

<u>3 1 4</u> 6 3 5 6 6

Multiplying the numbers of Caduceus yields us the most interesting set of numbers. $3 \times 1 \times 4 \times 6 = 72$. **72** is the number of years it takes for the stars to move one degree in the Precession of the Equinoxes (P.O.E.). $3 \times 1 \times 4 \times 6 \times 3 = $ **216**. 216 is nothing more than our holy number 108 x 2 and 216 times our base ten equals 2,160 or 1/12 our P.O.E. $3 \times 1 \times 4 \times 6 \times 3 \times 5 = $ **1,080** or 1/24 the Precession of the Equinoxes, as well as the radius of the Moon in miles. $3 \times 1 \times 4 \times 6 \times 3 \times 5 \times 6 = $ **6,480**, or 1/4 of the P.O.E. And lastly, $3 \times 1 \times 4 \times 6 \times 3 \times 5 \times 6 \times 6 - 38,880$, or one and a half cycles of the P.O.E.

By the precessional numbers we get from the numerical equivalent of Caduceus, it would seem that health and vitality is intimately linked to the Precession of the Equinoxes, the cosmic clock right above our heads.

THE LESSER WORK

To get a firm grasp on the alchemical process is next to impossible. So many of the alchemical illustrations and ideas varied from alchemist to alchemist and were shrouded in such symbolic meaning that for any one person to claim a complete understanding of it, would put them in the position of being highly suspect. One thing we can be certain of, though, is that in order to complete the alchemical work, one would need to focus on the compass, square and mathematics. Alchemists often spoke of two different aspects of the alchemical work, the Great Work and the Lesser Work. Most assuredly the Lesser Work had to be achieved in order to move on to the Great Work. So what is this "Lesser Work"?

The numerical equivalent of Lesser Work just might have our answer:

LESSER WORK
2 5 6 6 5 5 4 2 5 3 = **43**

The sum of "Lesser Work" equals 43. Besides being the 14th prime number, 43 has no particular qualities that we should draw our attention to but it is quite interesting what words and phrases share the sum of 43. "Tetractys", "Mathematics" and "Equilateral" all sum to 43, confirming our suspicions that in order to complete the Great Work, the Lesser Work would have to be done through the study of mathematics. Mathematics could help one understand one's "Mind Body and Soul" and quite possibly the "Holy Spirit".

MIND BODY AND SOUL   HOLY SPIRIT
1 5 1 4 2 2 4 2 1 1 4 6 2 6 2 = **43**   6 2 2 2 6 3 5 5 5 7 = **43**

"Apotheosis", or the Greek term for "man becoming divine", sums to 43 as well.

APOTHEOSIS
1 3 2 7 6 5 2 6 5 6 = **43**

Galileo exclaimed that "Mathematics is the language that God wrote the universe in." For the Greeks and the alchemists, understanding mathematics and the Tetractys was quintessential to understanding God. It was how God spoke to them. The Lesser Work was utilizing philosophy and mathematics to understand the monotheistic principles of the circle. The Great Work was going beyond number itself and finding oneself in the center of that circle.

THE GREAT WORK

The Great Work is the alchemical dream. It is the final product of one who engaged in the alchemical process and came to fruition as the fully developed, fully realized human being. The alchemist who finished the Great Work (though the Great Work in many ways can never truly be finished) became whole through his understanding of wholeness. He wore his spirit as he wore his flesh, he saw God in every nook and cranny, love in pain, perfection in flaws and was he who married his internal counterparts to become the wise sage and loving brother to all. The Great Work was the realization that nothing can be separated, that all is unified and therefore refusing another is refusing the self. The alchemist was the complete man. His wisdom did not come from being merely an intellectual, but from using every faculty at his disposal; intuition, ingenuity, creativity, imagination, rationale, reason and passion all played a part in completing the alchemical work. The alchemist understood that division from God was illusory. God was in every single thing and henceforth everything was God. And that of course, included the alchemist. The Great Work was this realization.

The numerical equivalent of the "Great Work" yields us the number **39**.

GREAT WORK
7 5 5 1 7 4 2 5 3 = **39**

"Root / Octave", "Sine / Cosine", "Freemasonry" and "Golden Rule" all sum to **39** as well.

The numerical equivalent of Christian also equals **39**.

CHRISTIAN
3 6 5 5 6 7 5 1 1 = **39**

In Christianity, the Lord's prayer speaks of "On Earth as it is in Heaven" and we often hear of "the kingdom of Heaven resides in you". Understanding these phrases fully is to understand the Great Work. Being a Christian is nothing more than saying "Christ I Am". No doubt this kind of thinking is blasphemous to the modern church, but is it so off base? One needs only to look to what Christ said himself for that answer.

"Whosoever drinks from my mouth *shall become as I am. I myself shall become that person* and the hidden things will be revealed."
- Gospel of Saint Thomas, *108*

The number 39 is of enormous significance. There are 39 categories of activity prohibited on Shabbat, 39 mentions of *work* or labor in the Torah, 39 books in the Old Testament according to Protestant canon, 39 statements on Anglican Church doctrine and there were 39 signers to the United States Constitution, out of 55 members of the Philadelphia Convention delegates. If we take our Holy Trinity and multiply it by our Rosicrucian 13, we yield the number 39. 39 is a most interesting number geometrically as well. 39 evenly spaced points on a circle can be connected by 13 equivalent lines.

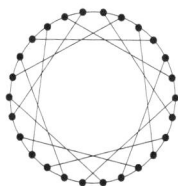

Completing the Great Work is awakening to the understanding that duality exists only in the material world and that the light and source that lie within each and every thing in the universe has no real divisions. Alchemy is the process of choosing to continually seek out the spiritual gold in the lead of one's material being. It is choosing to passionately seek out the pulse existing within the entirety of being and having *a direct experience with it*. It is the process of illuminating one's true identity.

The 39 equivalent edges as shown above can be viewed in two distinct different ways depending on one's perception.

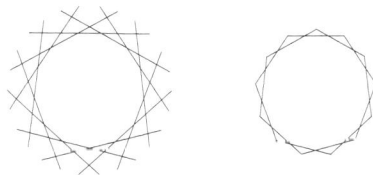

What do you see? The sticky traps of a web or a brightly beaming Sun?

In ancient Rome, the leaders of the Roman Catholic Church took their godhood to mean that they could induce punishment over those who did not understand or were not taught the secrets of their own divinity. They made the grandest of all mistakes and took *judgement* upon their fellow man. Citizens of Rome hit their slaves 39 times, referred to as "Forty save one".

JUDGEMENT

Many cultures, civilizations and religions throughout history believed in an afterlife. Many modern people see the idea of an afterlife as pure fantasy, crafted in the minds of primitive peoples as a way to cope with death. Losing a family member, friend or loved one can be excruciating and imagining them living on in some "better place" seems an apt way to deal with this pain psychologically. But is it that simple? The first law of thermodynamics states that energy can't be created or destroyed or, in other words, *energy can not die*. Though energy can't die, it can change from one form to another. The human body runs on this energy and it is what the ancients called a spirit or a soul. Where does this energy come from and where is it going? A common theme that is shared by many cultures is that when the person dies, this energy leaves the vehicle of flesh and moves on to higher or sometimes lower dimensions of being to either eventually rejoin the un-differentiated light of heaven or be reconstituted again in the lower realms. Upon death the soul undergoes a life-review and is judged for its actions on Earth. It is hard to imagine that we are given this gift of life and will not ultimately be held responsible for what we do with it while we are here. Are we free to do as we please without consequences? Are there rewards for those who do good deeds? Death is something we all must face. It is the one certainty in this life. No one gets out of here alive.

Mankind has placed many human characteristics upon God. God is either a vengeful, fearful God or a loving, caring and forgiving God. The alchemists and mystics of the past understood the folly in such thought. The Grand Architect, or THE ALL, as it is called by the Hermeticists, is all-encompassing and beyond the realms of duality. To THE ALL, good and evil are but equals, hanging fruit from the same tree. Good and evil are but one emotion on a varying scale. Upon being cast out of the Garden and into the material world, we were given the ability to see and choose what we wish to perceive. We were given the opportunity to find the balance on this widely varying scale. Do we choose the lead or the gold? Do we choose the good or do we choose the evil? Terence McKenna, a philosopher and ethnobotanist, once said "Upon death you will be condemned to live out the consequences of your tastes." If one understands that one is an "undivided section" of God and therefore an incarnate of this ultimate being, then it is easy to see that upon death, the person who will be doing the judging is none other than one's self.

The numerical equivalent of the word "judgement" sums to **40**.

JUDGEMENT
4 6 4 7 5 1 5 1 7 = **40**

There are 9 letters in judgement. 9 x 40 = 360. Since a circle encapsulates the greatest amount of space with its 360 degrees, it turns out that THE ALL, of which you are part, will be doing the judging. Your actions within the unity of all being *affect the entirety of being*. 40 has been a prominent number within scripture, mythology and folklore. Jesus fasted for 40 days and 40 nights before the temptation. Noah sailed for the same amount of time after the flood before landing and building civilization anew. Ali Baba of course had 40 thieves. 40 is an important number because it represents the equality and duality that exists between man and woman. Adam had 10 fingers and 10 toes and Eve had the same. Combining these two mythological characters, reflective of combining the opposites within the self, is the process undergone to achieve the Great Work. 40 is the ultimate number representing the conscious choices we make upon Earth. There are many important words that sum to 40;

Beautiful, Spiritual, Original Sin, Shepherd, Testament, Holy Ghost, Christmas, Rose Cross, Pythagoras

Judgement is not made of one's mistakes but how one learns from these mistakes. The alchemists speak about philosophical "gold" and we of course have the "Golden Rule":

Matthew 7:1 - Judge not, that ye be not judged.

"Rule" or "ruler" is a reference to measurement and so therefore judgement is measuring how much "gold" one brought to this great Earth. Finding balance and treating others as you wish to be treated is the only real "law" laid forth by the Great Spirit. Everyone is born into different circumstances. THE ALL recognizes every circumstance and understands the cards that each individual is dealt. The alchemical process is individualized for every soul born to this Earth. Playing the hand that one is dealt, even if the cards may seem stacked, is the object of the game. And ultimately, in this game of life, everyone can win if they play their cards right.

There is a scene sketched on one of the walls in the Great Pyramid of Giza that shows an Egyptian entering the afterlife and having his heart weighed on a scale with a feather, entitled "The Weighing of the Heart Ceremony". The message in this scene is intended to present the idea that if one's heart weighs less than a feather, then one is given the keys to the gates of Heaven. When the Egyptians embalmed the dead, they would perfectly preserve the body and many of the organs but would scoop out the brain entirely. This may in fact be a symbolic act to show the prominence of the heart. The brain and mind can trick oneself into believing all sorts of things, but the heart never steers one wrong. The human being can live on, albeit in a comatose state, if the brain has been damaged or destroyed but if the heart is destroyed, the soul must leave the body. As exclaimed before, the mystics understood that the real treasure lies in the chest of oneself. It is one's heart of gold. Follow your heart and it will not steer you wrong.

Judgement can be broken down in a myriad of interesting ways but we will focus on just two.

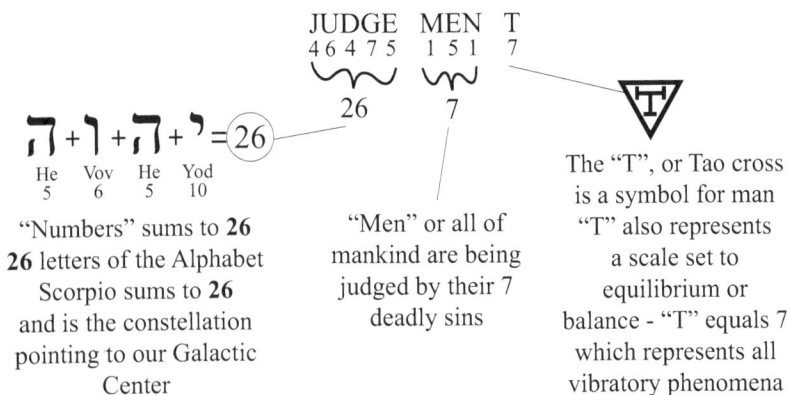

JUDGE MEN T
4 6 4 7 5   1 5 1   7

26   7

$$\daleth + \vav + \daleth + \yod = 26$$
He Vov He Yod
5   6   5   10

"Numbers" sums to **26**
26 letters of the Alphabet
Scorpio sums to **26**
and is the constellation
pointing to our Galactic
Center

"Men" or all of
mankind are being
judged by their 7
deadly sins

The "T", or Tao cross
is a symbol for man
"T" also represents
a scale set to
equilibrium or
balance - "T" equals 7
which represents all
vibratory phenomena

The JUDGE (represented by the Hebrew equivalent of the Tetragrammaton, the 26 letters of our alphabet and the SCORE **PI** O equaling 26 - pointing to the center of our galaxy) is judging MEN on how well balanced they were "T".

Since Shepherd equals 40 as well, let's break Judgement down using the Shepherd's cane, or the "J" as in "J"esus, as a mathematical tool to help us understand the numbers.

JUDGEMENT
4 6 4 7 5 1 5 1 7 = **40**

A 10
B 14
C 21
D 26
E 27
F 32
G 33
A 40

Shepherd's Cane
or the "J"

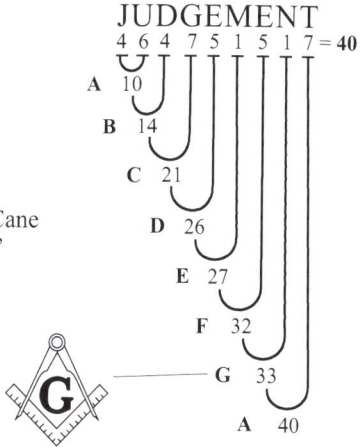

Using the symbol for "J", or a "fish hook", we can add the numbers of each individual letter together to find a new set of numbers encoded in the word Judgement. Each of these numbers is of grand significance in the language of mathematics and mythology. **10** is the base ten system, or Tetractys, **14** is the sections of Phi and Phee within the human body, as well as the number of stations of the cross in Jesus's Passion and the number of sections Osiris was cut into, **21** is the numerical equivalent of Queen and the multiplication of our hermaphroditic number 37 (3x7 = 21), **26** represents "Scorpio", "Center" the Hebraic Tetragrammaton and the Alphabet, **27** is the number of bones in the human hand, the numerical equivalent of "Light" and the mirror of 72, **32** and **33** represent the highest degrees in Freemasonry and **40** is of course, judgement.

Interestingly, if we assign each of these numbers notes from the musical scale, from root to octave, we find the number 33 is, not coincidentally, the letter "G"; A = 10, B = 14, C = 21, D = 26, E = 27, F = 32, **G** = **33**, A = 40. The highest degree the Mason may climb, or the 33rd degree, is just below the octave and ultimate judgement of oneself.

There are two different ways we may spell the word "Judgement", both of which are accepted in modern English. The Oxford English Dictionary prefers spelling the word with an "e", whereas the King James Bible spells it as "Judgment". Have we found ourselves at another crossroad?

One should immediately see that the letter "e" in the spelling of Judgement, lies in the middle of the word, almost as if to balance the four letters before it - "Judg" and the four letters after it - "ment". The letter "e" has a value of 5 and, as we have seen previously, the star pentagram encodes in its geometry the Golden Mean of 1.618. The word "mean" is defined as a balancing point. Interestingly, the lower case version of the Greek letter of Phee looks strikingly like a lower case "e" when mirrored and turned 90 degrees.

φ Phee ℮ "e"

Let's look at the numerical equivalent of the word "Judgment".

JUDGMENT
4 6 4 7 1 5 1 7 = 35

In the Egyptian "Weighing of the Heart Ceremony," one's "heart" is weighed against a "feather". This spelling of "judgment" and its numerical equivalent may help us to understand this myth a bit better.

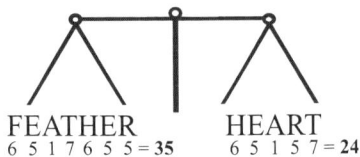

FEATHER   HEART
6 5 1 7 6 5 5 = 35   6 5 1 5 7 = 24

Notice "Feather" and "Judgment" both sum to **35**. In order to enter the gates of Heaven, one must find the Christ within him. We have seen that "Jesus Christ", "Alchemical Wedding", "Alchemical Marriage" and "The Holy Name of God" all sum to **59**. The 35 of "Feather" and the 24 of "Heart" added together find us, once again, that holy number **59**. "The Holy Name of God", therefore, is nothing more and nothing less than *your name*. So the question must be asked: Does your heart weigh less than a feather? We will explore this idea in depth in Volume 2 of this text.

THE PERENNIAL PHILOSOPHY

The Perennial Philosophy is the notion of the universal recurrence of philosophical insight independent of epoch or culture, including universal truths on the nature of reality, humanity or consciousness. Marsillo Ficino, Cicero and Aldous Huxley all spoke of and touted this mystical idea. The Perennial Philosophy expresses that inherent in nature exists a seed of knowledge that if found, could sprout the fundamental truths of the nature of creation. All those who sought it were worthy of the path but only those with a deep passion and commitment for truth were presented this high wisdom. The Perennial Philosophy is the story of the science of a universal religion that is shared by galaxies, stars, birds and people alike. Its song reverberates throughout the universe, its story told time and time again. And as we will see, this story of creation is reflected in the pro-creation of human beings.

The philosopher's egg, cosmic egg, primordial egg, primordial atom, Eye of Horus, Humpty Dumpty and the Garden of Eden are all references to the birth of creation. The egg from which you were born, nursed for 9 months in your mother's womb, is a reflection of the cosmic egg that birthed the universe. All of the potential energy in the universe was once encased inside the cosmic egg and upon the letting be of all light that potential coursed through space and time to create you. You are a reflection of the very first thing. Man is indeed *"made in the image of God"*.

In order to understand the birth of our universe, the first birth (or what is known by the Egyptians as the Zep Tepi, or "first time") or the *Virgin Birth,* we must also understand the birth of ourselves. The Holy Bible is an ancient book rich in symbolism, philosophical concepts, morality plays, mathematics and astral-theology but as a whole it is an allegory based entirely on the procreation of human beings.

A man and a woman come together through re-concilliation and unite in the act of making love. This passionate affair and the whirlwind surrounding it has been etched into poetry, spun into song and carved into trees throughout the centuries. Love, does in fact, make the world go round. Without the unification of opposites, mankind would cease to exist.

Love making the world go round is a sentiment expressed in the controversial line in the Bible saying: "Go fourth and multiply". The numerical equivalent of Multiply, *multiplied* equals 5,040, or the figure that emerges when one "Squares the Circle" of the Earth and the Moon whose combined radius equals 5,040 miles. This relationship of the Earth and the Moon in the Heavens is necessary to make our world go round. It is one of the great love affairs happening in our Solar System. Love is in fact what drives us nuts. It makes us *luna*tics.

The act of making love and thus *procreation* is easily symbolized by the Greek symbol and ratio of Phi and what we identified as the "Wholly" of a woman's vagina and the "Spear it" of a man's penis. This Holy Spirit is also expressed in the Greek Monad and Egyptian Sun glyph; a "whole" with the center "speared". Pi, with the "spear" of its diameter and the "wholly" of its circumference references this universal act as well.

A man's penis pierces or "spears" a woman's vagina or "wholly". When one of the man's sperm enters the egg and into the nuclei of the egg this "Holy Spirit" happens yet again. When the egg and sperm have combined, fertilization is thus complete. Conception begins when the father's sperm enters or cracks the mother's egg. It is in this very moment that two opposites combine, merging as one to start a new cycle of life. Conception begets us the mathematical paradox of sexual union itself: One man and one woman come together to become one. **1 + 1 = 1.** One sperm fertilizes one egg and becomes the conception of one child. Once again, **one + one = one.**

We have been told since childhood that one plus one will always equal two but that rule, in fact, doesn't apply when it comes to *you*, or the one who was birthed from the paradox of procreative mathematics. From the moment of conception, the form of the human vessel grows inside the waters of its creation, or our own mothers' wombs. This form grows from a perfect mathematical sequence of cell division called Mitosis. It may be interesting to note the similar sounds of *Mitosis, Isis,* and *Vesica Piscis.*

Mitosis, or the process of cell division throughout an impregnated woman's gestation cycle, begins when a man's sperm cracks the woman's egg. The initial egg separates creating two identical sets in two nuclei. From there, a doubling pattern commences to eventually form a newborn child in the womb. One cell divides to become 2. 2 becomes 4, 4 becomes 8, 8 becomes 16, 16 becomes 32, 32 becomes 64 and eventually after 9 months, the mother gives birth to one. And that one in your case, *is you*.

This doubling pattern that the cells undergo is reflected in the doubling and halving circuit of Marko Rodin's Vortex Based Math, utilizing the infinite number **64**, which is also the number of codons in DNA. Mitosis's pattern is also reflected in the Egyptian Eye of Horus myth as well as the famous Hermapolitan Mystery: "I am the one that becomes the two that becomes the four that becomes the eight that becomes one again." All of these concepts are referring to one thing and that is the mathematically perfect division of cells that eventually created you. The formation of the sacred geometrical "Seed of Life", echoing the 7 days of creation as well as the 6 dimensions of space, looks strikingly close to the phases of cell division (the first division is shown below).

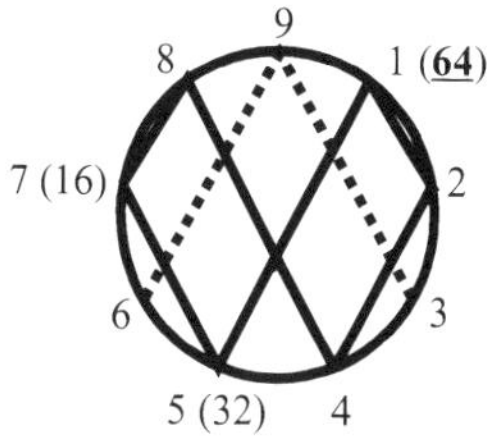

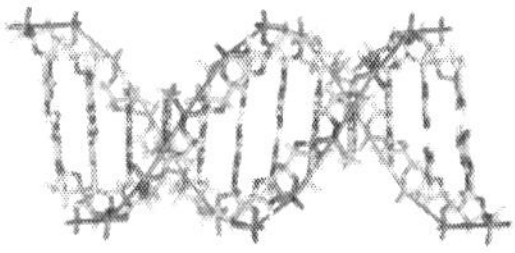

64 Codons of DNA

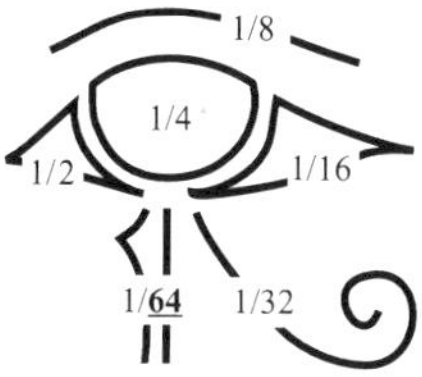

Sacred Geometrical Seed of Life

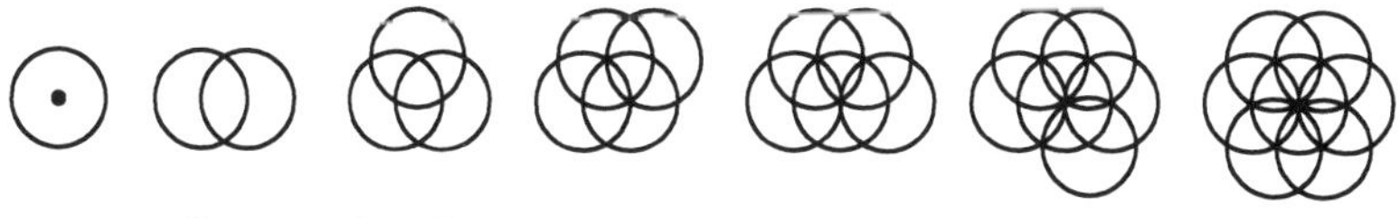

Constructing the "Seed of Life" - The 7 days of creation.

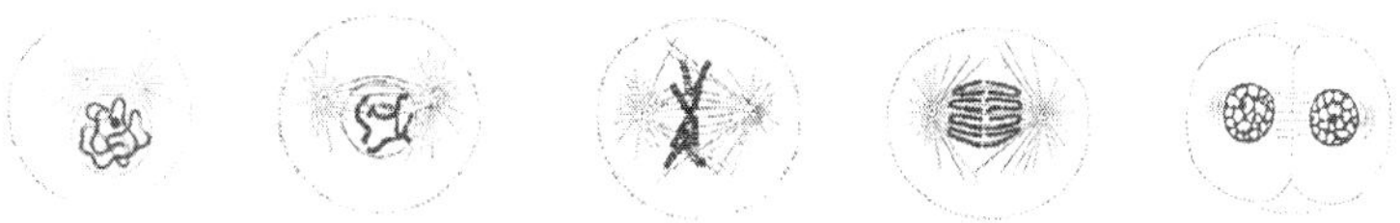

Phases of cell cycle and mitosis

To begin this process, first the man's sperm had to crack the woman's egg. The shape of a man's sperm is most revealing. Men's sperm resemble the shape of a snake or serpent.

According to the myth of the Garden of Eden, where the serpent tempted Adam and Eve, as well as according to the message left to us at Serpent Mound in Ohio, our primordial egg of creation's *fall*, or *crack,* was the result of an all powerful serpent. The primordial or cosmic egg represents the first thing in existence. It is our holy Pi. It is the sacred geometrical circular **3** of Heaven that one day cracked and sprouted the infinite digits of Pi. Since there could be nothing outside of this *first thing in existence*, in order for there to have been a Virgin Birth, a sperm or serpent would have to leave the egg, *cracking it from the inside.* We find this very thing in the Greek letter, Delta.

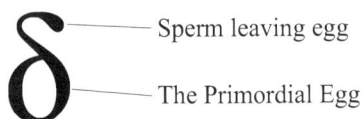

Sperm leaving egg

The Primordial Egg

This occurrence was, as we are told by Genesis, to be the result of original sin. This original sin or serpent that slithered out of our holy Pi, Garden of Eden or primordial egg is of course the mathematical "Origins of Sine". The serpent is the creature who separated us from ourselves, casting us out of our Garden of Even. Interesting to note though that it this very serpent who was powerful enough to convince us to commit such an act. This wise, crafty, slippery serpent we recognized as our spirit and taming or slaying that serpent as part of the alchemical goal. The temporary life that is given to us by our mothers cosmic egg and our father's serpent sperm is anchored in the realm of the ether. The ether was the 5th alchemical element to which all was connected. It was the great abyss from which we are born and to which we will return to upon death. The serpent tempted us into a world beyond the encasement of the ether of our primordial egg. It divided the first cell. It bore us into a world of opposites, of good and evil and most importantly, of life and death. Not realizing our true identify, our wholeness and unity of being has been our greatest sin ever since.

Adam and Eve's temptation and eating of the fruit of the knowledge of Good and Evil led to the fall of mankind, or the cracking of our cosmic egg. Getting back to the Garden is but to remind us that we are equals and but *shells* or *cells* of the cracked egg of our universe. Let's take a look inside the cosmic egg of creation or at the *chroma*somes that make up the *hue*man being.

Chromosomes can be divided into two types - autosomes and sex chromosomes. Certain genetic traits are linked to a person's sex and are passed on through the sex chromosomes, with the autosomes containing the rest of the genetic hereditary information. Human cells have 23 pairs of large linear nuclear chromosomes (22 pairs of autosomes and one pair of sex chromosomes) giving a total of 46 per cell.

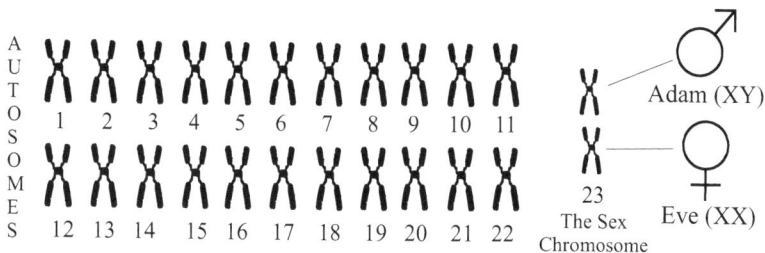

As we can see, this gives us 22 autosomes inside our cosmic egg, or Garden of Eden, with the last chromosome or sex chromosome being Adam and Eve. The sex of a human is noted by the symbols shown above as well as genetically by the XY for man and XX for woman. These 23 pairs of chromosomes *divide as well as multiply* in this first stage of creation, evident in the mathematics of Vortex Based math and mitosis. 23 is the numerical equivalent for *heaven*, *circle* and *temple*. These 23 pairs, giving us a total of **46,** yield us some very interesting correspondences for "The Holy Bible", the sacred geometrical "Seed of Life" and "Garden of Eden" all sum to **46**.

THE HOLY BIBLE	SEED OF LIFE	GARDEN OF EDEN
7 6 5 6 2 22 2 5 2 2 5 = 46	6 5 5 4 2 6 2 5 6 5 = 46	7 1 5 4 5 1 2 6 5 4 5 1 = 46

With *the application of mirroring*, this holy 46 encased inside our pri-mordial egg split. If we mirror this 46 it gives us 64, a number we've seen work its way into mitosis, the great Eye of Horus Myth and the slithering serpent-like strands of human DNA.

As a singular sex chromosome, Adam and Eve were *equals* in the Garden of Eden. They were a unified being at peace with 22 others. These 22 autosomes, or others, represent the Tree of the Knowledge of Good and Evil.

TREE
7 5 5 5 = **22**

But, as the story goes, one day a serpent came along with great power and tempted Adam and Eve to eat the "fruit" from the Tree of the Knowledge of Good and Evil. And so it was done.

FRUIT
6 5 6 5 7 = **29**

Tree, or **22,** plus Fruit, or **29,** equals **51**. 51 being the numerical equivalent of *Tetragrammaton, Universal Panacea,* and *Supreme Being.* The difference of 22 and 29 is SEVEN (Seven itself of course equaling 22 and encoding Pi) Isis equals **22** and Osiris equals **29**, together they are the *Fruit* (29) of the *Tree* (22) coming together as the *Supreme Being* (51). Isis divided by the difference of Isis and Osiris, or seven (29 - 22 = 7), again yields us Pi.

If we take the 22 autosomes as the Tree of Knowledge and divide it by the number of letters in the names of ADAM and EVE, or seven, we yield Pi. 22/7 = 3.142. Adam and Eve of course themselves together equal 22 and this divided by the 7 days of creation as well as by the 7 letters of their names yields us Pi. The 7 days of creation beginning with "God *saying* let there be *light!"* takes on a whole new meaning when one sees this light as the light of ones own *chroma*somes making up the vehicle of the *hue*man body.

There are 22 pair of autosomes, or **44** total, and therefore a pair of sex chromosomes being 2 make Adam and Eve. If we divide this sex chromosome, we yield two Adams and two Eves, or **14** letters total. 44/14 equals **3.142** or Pi. Eating the "apple" is what divided Adam and Eve from the rest of the 44. No doubt love and sex might of had something to do with it too.

APPLE	SEX	LOVE
1 33 2 5 = **14**	6 5 3 = **14**	2 2 5 5 = **14**

The 44 autosomes make up two trees of 22 or the two trees in the Garden of Eden; the Tree of Life and the Tree of the Knowledge of Good and Evil.

Females have two of the same kind of sex chromosome (XX), while males have two distinct sex chromosomes (XY). The numerical equivalents of these two chromosomes are interesting:

$$XY \quad XX$$
$$3\,2 \quad 3\,3$$

One should easily recognize the 32 and 33 degrees of Freemasonry encoded in these genetic letters. XY sums to 5 and XX sums to 6. 6/5 x 1.618 (Phi) squared equals 3.14159088... XY and XX added together equal Eleven. 11 once again is nothing more than an equal sign standing upright expressing that El is Even or *God is Even* giving us nothing more than the *Garden of Eden.* The numerical equivalent of Pi gives us the numbers 3 and 5.

$$PI$$
$$3\,5$$

If we place a decimal place between this 3 and 5, giving us **3.5,** and divide our Garden of Eden (11) by it, it once again yields us the holy ratio of Pi. 11 / 3.5 = 3.142. Or, better stated, XX + XY / P.I = **3.142**.

The most important thing about all this cracking of Pi is what it created and that is of course, *you.* Before we can get there though, we have to spend nine long months in the comfort and safety of our mothers' wombs.

Childbirth usually occurs about 38 weeks after conception and roughly 40 weeks from the start of the last normal menstruation. This time period is approximately **270** days. (270 / 7 is roughly 38.5 weeks). As we saw earlier the Hebrew numerical equivalent for INRI equaled **270**. (I - Yod = 10, N - Nun = 50, R - Resh = 200 and I - Yod = 10) A woman's gestation cycle (or the time period which you are in your mothers' womb) is the span of roughly nine months. If we highlight these nine months around our year of twelve months, we see that this period spans **270** degrees, or 3/4 of a circle.

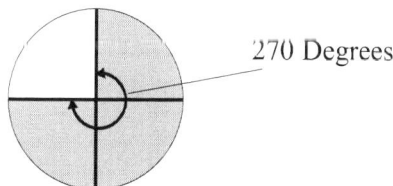

270 Degrees

30 days into the pregnancy the baby has eyes, ears, mouth, kidneys, liver, an umbilical cord and pumps its own blood. After 49 days (or 7 weeks of 7 days) a surge of energy ascends into the womb and it is then that the child develops not only its gender but its pineal gland. The pineal gland is the gland located in the center of one's head, nestled in the manger of the Thalamus. This gland is what is known as the third eye or brow chakra and actually has a cornea, lens and retina. Notice the **Pi** in pineal. "Pineal gland" adds up to one of the high degrees of spiritual enlightenment or 32.

PINEAL GLAND
3 5 1 5 1 2 7 2 1 1 4 = **32**

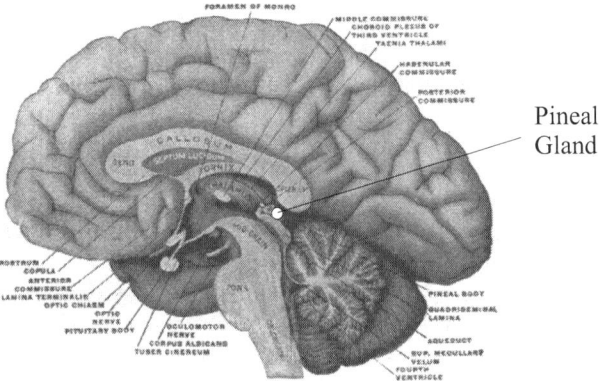

Pineal
Gland

This highly mystical organ's purpose is basically unknown, though Rene Descartes called it "the seat of the soul". It is the focus of much spiritual work as we are told in the Bible:

The light of the body is the eye: if therefore thine eye be single, thy whole body shall be full of light. ~ Matthew 6:22

The 49th day is recognized in our alphabet with each side of our alphabet summing to 49, or our central pillar of 7 squared (7 x 7 = 49) as well as referencing the Freemasonic symbol of the compass and square.

A B C D E F G H I J K L M
1 2 3 4 5 6 7 6 5 4 3 2 1 = **49**

 COMPASS   SQUARE
3 2 1 3 1 6 6   +   6 4 6 1 5 5 = **49**

Around eight weeks, the baby's cartilage skeleton begins to turn into bone and with the body essentially complete, the baby is now referred to as the foetus, which is Latin for "offspring". Notice foetus, has the smaller ratio of "Phee" in its pronunciation. Foetus in our cipher adds up to the high degree of 32.

FOETUS
6 2 5 7 6 6 = **32**

The stages of pregnancy are broken down into trimesters, or three months each. This separation of three is reflective of the Holy Trinity and the sacred geometrical 3 of Heaven. It is also reflective of the stages of life that the child will undergo once born; childhood, middle age and old age.

The development of brain cells, essential for higher functions, occurs during the tenth week or around day seventy. Within the next few months the baby starts to experience sensation. By month four, there is evidence that the foetus can hear sound and can even recognize its mother's voice. The child's heartbeat will even fluctuate when light is shone on the abdomen. In the fifth month, with the mother growing and showing considerably, the child has hair, eyebrows, eyelashes and nails. The baby usually starts kicking and movement in the womb is common. Throughout the following months both baby and mother physically and psychologically prepare for each other's arrival.

Within the last week of pregnancy the baby lies head downward since the head is usually the first part to emerge in birth. As labour begins, the mother's body prepares her with hormonal signals from the placenta. The uterus begins to contract and the neck of the womb, or cervix, slowly expands to allow axis for the baby to pass into the birth canal. When the amnion tears it releases a fluid referred to as "*the waters breaking*" and this is akin to the waters of creation pouring forth as the River of the Lord. Contractions become more frequent as the baby is pushed through the cervix and vagina but soon enough, a new baby is born. The umbilical cord is cut and the baby is presented to the nurturing arms of both its mother and of Mother Earth. The umbilical cord is symbolic of our link back to the creation and into the womb of our own cosmic egg of creation. The new born baby is a "Sun", or *divine child*, and is indeed born of the Holy Spirit, or the union of opposites.

A new child with **20** fingers and toes is born onto this Earth. From the depths of the unknown to the place we call home, a new "sun" is born. The number of days in a solar year, or **365.24** days is reflected in the numerical equivalent of CHILD.

CHILD
3 6 5 2 4 = **20**

365.24 days
in a Solar Year

Making love and bringing new life into the world is the one act shared by all of the peoples of the world. And as we have seen, we are but *reflections* of God, for indeed we are all but *children* of God.

GOD _____ CHILDREN
7 2 4 = **13** **31** = 3 6 52 4 5 5 1

Procreation can thus be seen as a *Great Work* of the true *Christian*.

PROCREATION
3 5 2 3 5 5 1 7 5 2 1 = **39**

GREAT WORK
7 5 5 1 7 4 2 5 3 = **39**

CHRISTIAN
3 6 5 5 6 7 5 1 1 = **39**

Procreation is not merely the act of making love with another but also the act of falling in love with yourself. The alchemical marriage was the consecration of this idea. Merging the opposites in oneself births a new-born "sun" or *reborn* man. Reborn with the knowledge that he is a per-fectly crafted individual, only divided from God by illusion. Yearning for this knowledge or gnosis, was to be *pro,* or for, the advancing of the *creation* of yourself. Not coincidentally, "*re-creation*" and "procreation" both equal **39**. The higher wisdom is to be sought within the self. Real-izing you are indivisible from the whole of being is the goal, *procreation, re-creation* or the transformation of the self is the path. Understanding that Jesus Christ, the Son of God, is but the Sun or great light of the spirit that lies within every child suddenly breathes new life into the famous line from John 14:6:

"Jesus saith unto him, I am the way, the truth, and the life: no man cometh unto the Father, but *by* me."

Enlightenment and recognizing the divine within is to be a Christ, a title available to every *child.*

THE HOLY GRAIL

The Holy Grail was known as the legendary cup from which Jesus drank, most notably at the Last Supper. This grail or cup was the highly sought after "object" in the Arthurian legends. "Holy Grail" sums to 32, representative of the 32 degrees in Freemasonic ascension.

HOLY GRAIL
6 222 7 5 1 52 = **32**

If we once again mirror our number line, as we did in the Garden of Eden, we can find the first 5 digits of Pi within both ends of our number line, these digits being, of course, mirrored.

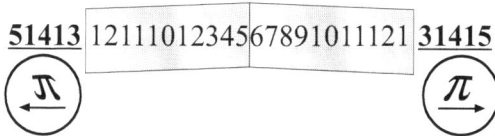

If we bring these two pi's, or two circles, together and join them in union, we can find the holy symbol of the Vescia Piscis.

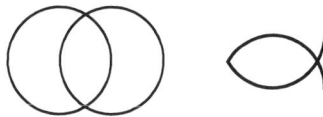

As we have said, the Vesica Piscis is the symbol from which the Jesus fish originated. The symbol of the motherly Vescia Piscis encodes not only the womb of all creation, but the "Sun" of God as well. The fish symbol recognized in the constellation Pisces, or "two fish", is a creature often used in the mythologies of many cultures. The Dogon tribe of Africa celebrate a "Nummo" fish and in the Egyptian myth of Isis and Osiris, Set cast one of Osiris's pieces into the Nile river only to be eaten by a *fish*. Current evolutionary theory believes that mankind crawled onto land as a fish in the Devonian era. In early Christianity, this fish was drawn by two Christians, signifying the unity of opposites; one person drew the left side and the other drew the right. The sum of the numbers of "fish" equal, not coincidentally, **23**, the numerical equivalent of *heaven, circle* and *temple*,

FISH
6 56 6 = **23**

114

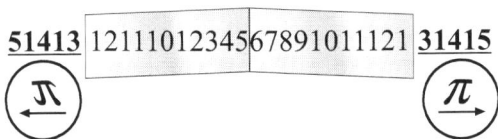

51413 12111012345|67891011121 **31415**

If we add up these 5 digits of Pi, they equal **14**. (3+1+4+1+5=**14**). These "mirrored Pis", both equaling 14, represent your symmetrical hands. Look down at your hands and count the 14 sections of your 4 fingers and thumb on each hand.

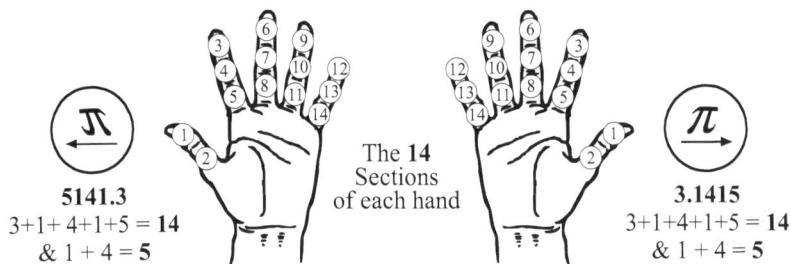

5141.3
3+1+ 4+1+5 = **14**
& 1 + 4 = **5**

The **14** Sections of each hand

3.1415
3+1+4+1+5 = **14**
& 1 + 4 = **5**

If you notice, using Pythagorean addition and adding the 1 and 4 in **14**, this yields us **5**, *or the 14 sections of your hand making up 5 fingers.* The 5 fingers on your left hand and the 5 fingers on your right hand come together in the act of prayer, thus merging the opposites. If we mirror the symbol for **5** and put it together, we yield a symbol that looks strikingly like a cup.

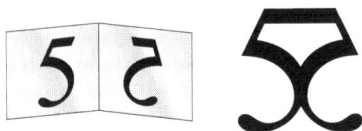

The mythical, all-powerful magic cup from which Jesus drank was none other than his own hands. The riddle encoded in this myth carries with it a powerful message: *We all carry the Holy Grail for we are all divine.*

Much like the alchemical Philosopher's Stone, The Holy Grail was not an artifact to be found, buried 'neath the sands of history but instead a cosmic truth to be discovered within oneself. Your own hands can be used to drink up the holy waters of creation for you are indeed a "Sun" of God.

ENLIGHTENMENT

Enlightenment means illumination. It means the spiritual rebirth of one's self. Illumination is available for all those who seek it. Becoming enlightened is fully understanding the Hermetic maxim of "As above, so below." The entire cosmos, from the Sun and Moon to the stars above, *from your perspective*, revolves around *you*. The Thrice-Great Hermes Trismegistus exclaimed; "God is an infinite sphere, the center of which is everywhere, the circumference nowhere." Make no mistake about it, the center in which Hermes speaks of is *you*. This idea is encoded within the Greek Monad and Egyptian sun glyph reminding us that we are indeed the "Suns" of God.

The numerical equivalents of "circumference", "enlightenment", "Vesica Piscis", the Freemasonic "Supreme Council" and "Christianity" are most interesting.

CIRCUMFERENCE   ENLIGHTENMENT   VESICA PISCIS
3 55 3 6 1 6 5 5 5 1 3 5 = **53**   5 1 2 5 7 6 7 5 1 1 5 17 = **53**   5 5 6 5 3 1 3 5 6 3 5 6 = **53**

SUPREME COUNCIL   CHRISTIANITY
6 6 3 5 5 1 5 3 2 6 1 3 5 2 = **53**   3 6 5 5 6 7 5 1 1 5 7 2 = **53**

If we utilize the mathematics of the symbol of the holy cross (multiplication: X and addition: +) and multiply **5 x 3**, we get **15**. If we add 5 + 3 we get **8**. **15 + 8** yields us nothing more than **23**, the numerical equivalent of *heaven, circle, temple, natural* and *beauty*.

With the application of mirroring, 53 now becomes 35. Pi gives us the numbers **3** and **5**. Three very important words sum to **35**.

53 | 35

PI   ILLUMINATI   JERUSALEM   GENESIS
35   5 2 2 6 1 5 1 1 75 = **35**   4 5 5 6 6 1 2 5 1 = **35**   7 5 1 5 6 5 6 = **35**

Illumination is for the attainment of all and is certainly not intended for but a mere select few. The Holy Land lies within the self and this truth will live on. For each "human being" is an aspect of the living God.

HUMAN BEING
6 6 1 1 1 2 5 5 1 7 = **35**

Pi represents nothing more and nothing less than the circumference of our entire universe. The reason we cannot fully comprehend Pi is because we can not truly measure the circumference of the universe. The famous mathematician Kurt Goedel reminded us of this fact by his "Incompleteness Theorem".

"Anything you can draw a circle around cannot explain itself without referring to something outside the circle – something you have to assume but cannot prove."

Pi, as we know, is the ratio of a circle's circumference to its *diameter*. The numerical equivalent of diameter is most interesting.

DIAMETER
4 5 1 1 5 7 5 5 = 33

Diameter means to "measure twice". We create Pi with a compass, which means we use the *radius to find the diameter*. Therefore the diameter is in fact instructing us to *measure the radius twice*. The plural of radius is RADII. We can de-construct the word radii once again using the fourth letter of our alphabet or D.

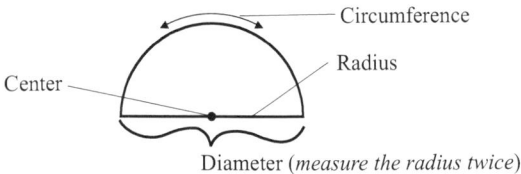

Diameter (*measure the radius twice*)

Notice in the word RADII, we have RA, the Egyptian Sun God, the letter "D" giving us the mathematics necessary to find Pi as well as two letter "I's". These two "I's" represent the two radii, one male and one female. They are Adam and Eve, Isis and Osiris and the hero twins in the ancient Mayan myth of "One-hunhapu". These twins are also represented by the constellation of The Twins, or Gemini. If we break apart the word "Gemini" we reveal the true message of this constellation - GEM IN I. The spirit and light of creation, or the **GEM**, is within you.

These two "Is" also represent the two "eyes" in your very head.

117

When one undergoes the process of merging the opposites that exist within the self, they become one with the "All Seeing "**I**" of God. These two radius merge as the diameter, creating a single line, or I, representing the alchemical marriage. This "I" also represents the primordial scission of our cosmic egg or the cracking of Pi. It is "I" that *divided the circle*. Becoming truly holy, or finding the wholeness within the self is the act of piecing back together our cosmic egg. It is the act of finding the divine by sewing up the divide of Pi. This simple truth is, once again, expressed in the symbol of the Greek Phi, or Golden Mean.

$$\Phi$$

This symbol seems to say *"I divide the circle"*. The ratio of Phi exists all throughout nature and this simple ratio expresses the growth, balance and spiral nature of all things. We are born of this ratio and we will die by its hands. With the credo of "I divide the circle" we can understand that we are but a fraction, a being cracked from our primordial egg. *We are the "I" that divided the circle. We are the diameter needed to find the ratio of Pi.*

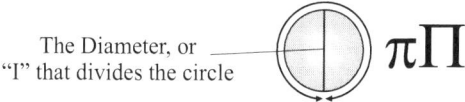

The Diameter, or
"I" that divides the circle

The Eye of Providence or the All-Seeing Eye of God is often recognized as the ultimate symbol of illumination. The All Seeing Eye of God atop the pyramid represents you. At the Great Pyramid of Giza, the capstone is missing and many claim there may never have been one in the first place. If we utilize our gematria rule of "coming up one short" we can realize the symbolism of this *"missing"* capstone. Was there ever a capstone on the pyramid? If there was, how was it lost? The missing capstone represents you, the missing *one*. *You* are the All-Seeing Eye of God in the capstone elevated atop of the pyramid. This position comes with much responsibility and many hardships but its rewards are even greater. Do not forget your rightful place on this pyramid of existence.

"The New World is being Ordered by those who know numbers. If we let others control our numbers, we will banish ourselves from the Garden of Even." ~ Claudia Pavonis

AS ABOVE, SO BELOW

The most famous of the Hermetic maxims is "As above, so below". Countless other religions and spiritualities have echoed this sentiment and there is good reason why. Like in a hologram, within every part lies a reflection of the whole. The modern day understanding of fractals, a beautiful mathematical model of this philosophy, helps us understand the very nature of being. Within the microcosm reflects the macrocosm. Within the very small lies a reflection of the very big. This is the way the Grand Architect works its magic within the natural world.

If this philosophy and scientific observation is correct, we should find the same phenomena in the numerical equivalent of "As above, so below".

AS ABOVE   SO BELOW
1 6 1 2 2 5 5 = **22**   6 2 2 5 2 2 4 = **23**

Accordingly, "As above" should be numerically equivalent to "so below" but this is not what we find. "As above" sums to 22 and "so below" sums to 23. A difference of *one*. It seems that we have "come up one short". The sum of "as above" divided by its 7 letters yields us Pi. 22/7 = 3.142. The 23 of "So below" we recognize as the numerical equivalent of *circle*, *heaven* and *temple*. That *temple* being your very body.

As it turns out, the Great Pi in the Sky, or "As above", does in fact equal the "So below" of the Heaven found right here on Earth.

| Pi
3.142...
"As above" | Sacred
geometrical
Heaven
"So below" | Lakota symbol for
"As above, so below". | Jewish
Star of David
symbol for
"As above, so below." |

"That which is in the stars is also on the Earth and that which is on the Earth is also in the stars." - Lakota saying

"Thy kingdom come. Thy will be done in earth, as *it is* in heaven."
- Matthew 6:10

MONOMYTHTICISM

The American author Willa Cather once said "There are only two or three human stories, and they go on repeating themselves as fiercely as if they had never happened before." James Joyce echoed that sentiment and embedded it in his novel *Finnegan's Wake,* an amalgamation of all time into one story. Ultimately, the universe is unified and must be born of a single story. The universe tells us this truth by its very name; *uni* means "one" and *verse* means a "line of poetry". All religions, at their heart, are telling this same poetic story. Religion comes from the Sanskrit word *religio.* "Ligio" means a link of chain, a yoke or union and "re" means "back" or "to bind". The practice of religion is therefore the intention of *linking onself back* to the creator and the first moments of creation. Spiritual practice is meant to help one understand that the story of the universe is *your story*; a story of the singularity within the absolute wholeness and the wholeness within the singularity. A profound truth that the poet William Blake tried to inform us of in the opening lines of "Auguries of Innocence":

> To see a world in a grain of sand,
> And a heaven in a wild flower,
> Hold infinity in the palm of your hand,
> And eternity in an hour

A story and philosophy expressed in the simplest of symbols.

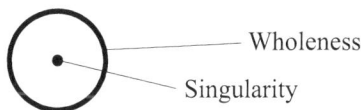

And yet it is all too often, and quite a shame, that many modern religions have us running around in circles instead of leading us to their centers.

The peoples of the past left us clues to help us find our place in this cosmos. A reality in which man is not against nature but instead an intimate part of the beauty of its cycles and workings. By using every faculty we have at our disposal, utilizing every tool in our chest, by becoming explorers of the mind and warriors of the heart, we can carve a new path out of the darkness of the woods and into the clearing of pure spirit. The heroes, saints, magis, philosophers and sages of the past reminded us that it is our rightful place on this pyramid of existence.

There is only one God and one story. This one, or *mono,* story, or *myth,* can be intuitively grasped by the power of the *mystic* properties of number, symbolism and language. And ultimately, through understanding *oneself.*

Buried within the spirit of the Earth exists a germinal seed of truth. It is a seed born from the stars that has but one story to tell and yet tells that story in infinitely numinous ways. Throughout history many tribes, cultures and civilizations have crafted its magic into art, architecture, song, dance, nursery rhymes and rituals but most importantly, this seed of knowledge was sewn into myth through the art of the parable. A parable is a story that strikes the heart of the imagination and is intended to compel one to question the *mystery* of being. A parable can also lead one to the answer of that mystery. For the answer to the "mystery" of this universe is *within us.* Or as J.J. Van der Leeuw exclaimed, "The real mystery of life is not a problem to solve, it is a reality to be experienced." The "*mystery*" is indeed "*mystory*".

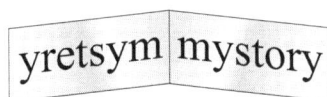

yretsym mystory

Mythologies are how our ancestors passed down the high wisdom and knowledge of their ages to us. Understanding the messages encoded within these stories and intuiting their knowledge into one's own life can help signify a "spiritual rebirth" by understanding the *natural religion* that exists within all. Parables are presented to one in the forms of riddles because one he who seeks to know the answer to the *riddle* of this life will end up looking deep within himself and past the surface meaning of our myths. Encoding the riddle of existence into the riddle of parables is the best way to pass on the hidden magical truths of being. Jesus Christ himself told us of this fact:

"And the disciples came, and said unto him, *Why speakest thou unto them in parables?* He answered and said unto them, Because it is given unto you to know the mysteries of the kingdom of heaven, but to them it is not given. For whosoever hath, to him shall be given, and he shall have more abundance: but whosoever hath not, from him shall be taken away even that he hath. Therefore speak I to them in parables: because they seeing see not; and hearing they hear not, neither do they understand."
~ Matthew 13:10 - 13

"I have said, Ye are gods; and all of you *are* children of the most High."
~ Psalm 82:6

APPRECIATION

A deep appreciation goes out to all the researchers, new and old, whose work I profited from. I am, and will always be, but a student learning from the masters around me. There have been countless people who have contributed ideas, via the internet, as well as in my personal life, which led me to further discoveries and without these, this book could never have happened. Though too numerous to name, a heartfelt thanks goes out to all of them. A few people and organizations must be noted though:

Scott Onstott, Santos Bonacci, Johan Oldenkamp, Henrik Palmgren and all the folks at Red Ice Creations, Ruth Smith (for supporting independent researchers), Paul Fix (for the 47 degrees), Marko Rodin, Randy Powell, Gray Scott at Serious Wonder, Dennis Fetcho at Inside the Eye Live, all the folks at Image King Signs, the good folks in Jamalia (It was one of the pleasures of my life meeting all of you. I will be forever blessed for our time together - Long Live Jamalia!), Judd Sawyer (for your warm heart and Bear Creek), The Huber Music Company and the Royal Terror Theatre (for the best friends and creative outlets a guy could ask for), Dylan O'Fallon (for the late night conversations), Thomas and Melea Roed (for showing me what *real people* look like), Toby Kubler (for the even later night conversations), Dave Waller (for showing me that growing up isn't giving up), the Grubers, Star Davis-Swan, the Anderson and Lawrence families, Vincent and Leticia Respa (for the Isolation Tank and welcoming me into your home) and the editor Alison Dasho.

Thank you to all who have supported me over the years and my sincerest apologies if I have forgotten any of you.

And much thanks to all the characters in my life, real and imagined.

And to all the alchemists whose names I'll never know.

A very special thanks to my family. Thanks for putting me on the ground and keeping me grounded. I love you.

And lastly, to the peacock. Love is like pi: Infinite, transcendental and often considered irrational. Thank you for making me whole. I love you.

RAHFI BLU PFEUTI

Spin me a yarn and tell me a tale
Place me in the belly of a big fat whale
Find me a vessel and set it to sail
Sing me a song for to jump and to wail
For Philos and Christos may very well do!
But what is so wrong with the name that is you?

Weave me of cloth and craft me a dress
Dance me along for it is we that are blessed
Find me a path where no sun sets West
Sew up the divide in the divine of my chest
For Philos and Christos may very well do!
But what is so wrong with the name that is you?
Nothing I say!
Yours will do too!
But the name that was given is
Rahfi Pfeuti Blu

RAHFI	BLU	PFEUTI
5 1 6 65 = **23**	2 2 6 = **10**	3 6 5 6 7 5 = **32**

23 = Heaven , Circle, Natural, Beauty, Temple

Tetractys

(365) Solar Year

π The name Pfeuti is similar to that of Christ; both equaling 32 and both names beginning with the 365 days of our solar year. Rahfi and Blu added together make 33, giving us the 32 and 33 degrees of spiritual enlightenment. Notice the sun God "Ra" as well as the ratio of "Phee" in the name. Blue is a color adored by the Egyptians and Mayans that represented the waters of creation and the great potential or "blue sky" that exists within mankind. Rahfi Blu Pfeuti adds to **65**. The first nine numbers of Pi ending in **65**, or 3.14159265, added together equal **36**, representing the 360 degrees of a circle. These 9 digits multiplied to- gether give us the number 32,400, or one and one quarter turn on our zodiacal clock.

THE COSMIC PRINCIPLES

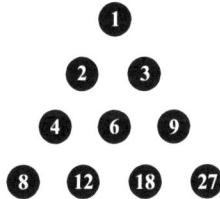

The Pythagorean Tetractys

Monad - 1) The first number in existence, self-replicating, contains all potential, androgynous in nature. Greek = 361. Features: divine, intellect, wisdom, what is equal among greater and lesser, singularity and wholeness

Dyad - 2) Duality, Unity of Opposites, The first even number, creation of a line - two points, division / multiplication / addition, generation. Features: indivisible equality, movement towards being.

Triad - 3) The Trinity, the source of all actuality in number, creation of space, sacred geometrical Heaven / Circle. First truly odd number. 3 kinds of triangles - equilateral, isosceles and scalene, 3 rectilinear angles - acute, obtuse and right. Features: beauty, fairness, perfection, unification, harmony.

Tetrad - 4) Sacred geometric Earth, square, volume. Four foundations of wisdom: arithmetic, music, geometry and astronomy, ordered 1, 2, 3 and 4. Four directions, elements and seasons - Earth, Fire, Air, Water / North, East, West and South / Winter, Spring, Summer, Autumn.

Pentad - 5) Phi, The Mean or balancing point, 5 Platonic solids - Tetrahedron Hexahedron, octahedron, isocahedron, dodecahedron. 5 extensions of the human body, 5 senses. Knitting together of odd and even (2 and 3)

Hexad - 6) A "perfect" number consisting of the divisions of 1/3, ½ and 1/6. 6 dimensions of space, 6 is the perfect form and the geometry of "as above, so below". Organizing principle. Six zodiacal signs are over our Earth and six are under the Earth.

Heptad - 7) Seven: notes of the major scale, colors of the Rainbow, days of creation, chakras, days in the week, deadly sins. Seven types of geometric names: point, line, surface, angle, shape, solid, plane.

Octad - 8) 6th number of the Fibonacci sequence. Even slices of a Pi! Mobius strip and infinity. The square root of 64. The octave.

Ennead - 9) The Horizon, last odd number in the base 10 system, "666". The serpent.

Decad - 10) Completion, The Tetractys, Base ten system. Fingers on a human being.

HELPFUL RESOURCES

FIBONACCI NUMBERS

0, 1, 1, 2, 3, 5, 8, 13, 21, 34, 55, 89, 144, 233, 377, 610, 987, 1597, 2584,
4181, 6765, 10946, 17711, 28657, 46368, 75025, 121393, 196418, 317811...

PRIME NUMBERS

2, 3, 5, 7, 11, 13, 17, 19, 23, 29, 31, 37, 41, 43, 47, 53, 59, 61, 67, 71, 73, 79,
83, 89, 97, 101, 103, 107, 109, 113, 127, 131, 137, 139, 149, 151, 157, 163,
167, 173, 179, 181, 191, 193, 197, 199, 211, 223, 227, 229, 233, 239, 241,
251, 257, 263, 269, 271, 277, 281, 283, 293, 307, 311, 313, 317, 331...

THE HEBREW ALPHABET

א	ב	ג	ד	ה	ו	ז	ח	ט
Aleph = 1	Beth = 2	Gimel = 3	Daleth = 4	He = 5	Vau = 6	Zayin = 7	Cheth = 8	Teth = 9

י	ך כ	ל	מ	נ	ס	ע	פ
Yod = 10	Kaph = 20	Lamed = 30	Mem = 40	Nun = 50	Samech = 60	Ayin = 70	Pe = 80

צ	ק	ר	ש	ת
Tsaddi = 90	Koph = 100	Resh = 200	Shin = 300	Tau = 400

The Finals

ך	ם	ן	ף	ץ
Koph = 500	Mem = 600	Nun = 700	Pe = 800	Tsaddi = 900

THE GREEK ALPHABET

Αα	Ββ	Γγ	Δδ	Εε	Ζζ	Ηη	Θθ	Ιι
Alpha - 1	Beta - 2	Gamma - 3	Delta - 4	Epsilon - 5	Zeta - 7	Eta - 8	Theta - 9	Iota - 10

Κκ	Λλ	Μμ	Νν	Ξξ	Οο	Ππ	Ρρ
Kappa - 20	Lambda - 30	Mu - 40	Nu - 50	Xi - 60	Omicron - 70	Pi - 80	Rho - 100

Σσς	Ττ	Υυ	Φφ	Χχ	Ψψ	Ωω
Sigma - 200	Tau - 300	Upsilon - 400	Phi - 500	Chi - 600	Psi - 700	Omega - 800

REFERENCES & SOURCES

All pictures and illustrations - www.wikipedia.com
All etymology - www.etymonline.com
All other illustrations / graphics created by Marty Leeds
Cover Page Illustration - "Squaring the Circle"
by Michael Maier, Scrutinium Chymicum
"Squaring the Circle" explanation, page 14, from Stephen Skinner's "Sacred Geometry"
Torus images borrowed from www.theharmonicresonance.com
"Silver Fraction", page 69, borrowed from Richard Heath and John Michell's "The Lost Science of Measuring the Earth"
"Perfect Pythagorean Triangle" page 69, borrowed from "Sun, Moon and Earth" by Miranda Lundy
"The Primordial Egg" explanation, page 90, borrowed from www.wikipedia.com
Cross-scetion of DNA, page 94, courtesy of Dr. Robert Langridge
Page 122: Illustration by Jacob Boehme (1575 - 1624)

The following is a suggested reading list. An extra special thanks goes out to all of these fantastic researchers. Many of the concepts, ideas and philosophies within this volume were inspired by these works:

The Holy Bible - King James Version, Masonic Edition
A History of God - Karen Armstrong
Finnegans Wake - James Joyce
Te Tao Ching - Lao Tzu
Psychology and Alchemy - Carl Jung
Modern Man in Search of a Soul - Carl Jung
Man and His Symbols - Carl Jung
The Light of Egypt, Volume 1 & 2 - Thomas Burgoyne
God-Man: The Word Made Flesh - George W. Carey and Inez Eudora Perry
The Alvin Boyd Kuhn Collection - Alvin Boyd Kuhn
The Esoteric Structure of the Alphabet and its Hidden Mystical Language- Alvin Boyd Kuhn
Sacred Geometry - Stephen Skinner
Quadrivium (The Four Classic Liberal Arts of) - Keith Critchlow, Miranda Lundy, David Sutton, Jason Martineau, John Martineau Anthony Ashton

Useful Mathematical & Physical Forumlae - Matthew Watkins
A Study of Numbers - R.A. Schwaller de Lubicz
The Theology of Arithmetic (Iamblichus) - Translated by Robin Waterfield
The Corpus Hermeticum - Translated by G.R.S. Mead
The Emerald Tablet of Hermes and The Kybalion - Edited by Dr. Jane Ma'ati
Smith C. Hyp. Msc. D.
The Secret Doctrine - Helena Blavatsky
The Secret Teaching of all Ages - Manly P. Hall
The Lost Keys of Freemasonry - Manly P. Hall
Sun, Moon and Earth - Robin Heath
The Science of the Dogon - Laird Scranton
The Cosmological Origin of Myth and Symbol - Laird Scranton
Myths to Live By - Joseph Cambell
The Hero With a Thousand Faces - Joseph Cambell
Lost Star of Myth and Time - Walter Cruttendon
Serpent In The Sky - John Anthony West
Aerodynamics Point Energy Creation Physics - Marko Rodin
Signs and Symbols - DK Publishing
The Lost Masonic Word - Dr. J.D. Buck
Through Indian Eyes, The Untold Story of Native American Peoples -
Editors of Reader's Digest
Lakota Star Theology, Studies in Lakota Stellar Theology - Ronald Goodman
Man's Search for Meaning - Viktor E. Frankl
Science and the Akashic Field - Ervin Laszlo
A Beginner's Guide to Constructing the Universe - Michael S. Schneider
How the World is Made - John Michell with Allan Brown
The Lost Science of Measuring the Earth - John Michell and Robin Heath
Knowledge of Higher Worlds and its Attainment - Rudolf Steiner
On Formally Undecidable Propositions of Principia Mathematica and
Related Systems - Kurt Goedel
Religion in the Making - Alfred North Whitehead
Pythagoras - Thomas Stanley
The Phenomenon of Man - Pierre Teilhard de Chardin
The Holy Science - Swami Sri Yukteswar
The Egyptian Book of the Dead - Chronicle Books
Alan Watts - This is It
Siddartha - Herman Hesse
God Has a Dream - Desmond Tutu
The Archaic Revival - Terence McKenna
The Gnostic Circle - Patrizia Norelli Bachelet
In a Sacred Manner I Live, Native American Wisdom - Edited by Neil Philip

A History of Western Philosophy - Betrand Russell
Wholeness and the Implicate Order - David Bohm
Cosmic Trigger - Robert Anton Wilson
The War of Art - Steven Pressfield
The Secret Language of Birthdays - Gary Goldschneider

Lectures, Videos and Online Sources:

Secrets in Plain Sight - Scott Onstott, www.secretsinplainsight.com
Santos Bonacci - Lecture Series, www.universaltruthschool.com
Various lectures - "The Psychedelic Salon" with host Lorenzo
Johan Oldenkamp - Lecture Series, www.pateo.nl
Magical Egypt - John Anthony West
Maybe Logic - Robert Anton Wilson
The Cross of Thoth - Crichton E. Miller
Joseph Cambell, Collected Lectures and The Power of Myth with Bill Moyers
www.jcf.org
Nassim Haramein - http//:theresonanceproject.org
Northern Exposure Television Series
www.wikipedia.com
http://alanwatts.com - Alan Watts, Life and Works
www.schooloftheholyscience.org
www.khanacademy.org
http://vihart.com - Vi Hart, Mathemusician

Also available from Marty Leeds:
Pi - The Great Work
Please visit: www.martyleeds33.com

5210190R00080

Printed in Great Britain
by Amazon.co.uk, Ltd.,
Marston Gate.